Bumps On The Road To Riches

*How to Avoid the Big Mistakes That Kill
Small Businesses*

Jim Olsztynski

DEDICATION

Dedicated to all the under-appreciated craft workers and contractors who build, maintain and repair the structures, equipment and systems that make our lives healthy and comfortable.

CONTENTS

ACKNOWLEDGMENTS

This is the hardest section of this book for me to write, because inevitably I will leave out the names of many people who have contributed most of the information in this book. This includes numerous friends and colleagues with whom I have worked over the years, along with hundreds of business owners and managers whose organizations I have written about. Given sufficient time and thought I could probably fill a dozen pages with names of these individuals, some of whom may not even remember me or know that they provided me with memorable insights.

Instead, I'm going to be picky and single out only a few people whose lessons play out again and again throughout this book. First and foremost among them is my original boss and mentor in the trade publishing field, the late Charlie Horton. Charlie taught me always to respect people who earned their livings doing grubby and grueling work, and to use my talents to spotlight their under-appreciated activities. He also was the best writer I'd ever known – until Dan Holohan came along.

Dan Holohan's prolific prose harnesses technical knowledge, marketing savvy, wit and soulfulness to shed light on the human condition in the business world. Nobody has a keener eye for detail or better insights into what makes people and things work the way they do

Ellen Rohr is another name that pops up several times in this book. Her business experience combines with an ebullient personality to make her Ms. Can Do! I am especially grateful for Ellen's extensive and thoughtful comments in helping to edit this book.

Nobody has contributed as much sheer business wisdom as Frank Blau, whose mentoring has lifted thousands of men and women from the dregs of business ownership to the peaks of success. Most of what I've written about the importance of numbers crunching comes from Frank Blau's fertile brain.

Finally, I'd like to single out Al Levi, whose common-sense business philosophies have imbedded in my mind. If I were starting a new business, I'd want Al to run it or at least help set up its operations.

INTRODUCTION

Small businesses are the backbone of our economy. During a career spanning more than three decades as a trade magazine editor and writer, my job was to study and write about what made predominantly small businesses tick. Along the way I got to know thousands of business owners and their associates, and am fortunate to count hundreds of them as friends. Studying and befriending them for so many years, I grew to appreciate small business owners and managers for the risks they take, for the long hours they put in, for how hard they work, for their expertise in various fields, and not least for providing livelihoods for so many employees.

Many of the thousands of business owners I met had brilliant business sense, and quite a few of them got rich as a result. Others went broke. Occasionally someone went broke despite being brilliant, either because s/he made mistakes or because lady luck turned fickle. I've learned that luck often trumps brilliance. It's hard to overcome being in the wrong place or the wrong market at the wrong time.

The flip side is that it's hard NOT to make money when you're in the right place and the right market at the right time. I saw a lot of that in the construction and construction services industry, where I spent my career.

The quarter-century stretching from 1983 to 2007 saw the greatest construction boom ever in the United States, with a couple of short-lived recessionary setbacks sprinkled in. During that time contractors found themselves turning down a lot of jobs because they didn't have enough crews to handle them or they were picky about choosing the most profitable work, as they should. The leftovers were sufficient to feed thousands upon thousands of independent craftsmen who could find enough work to make a living based on their craft skills, but who were clueless about running a business enterprise. They landed jobs almost solely through bottom-feeder pricing and most had business practices to match. Market pricing got squeezed so that even during the boom times, one of the biggest complaints of construction contractors was low profit margins. Then the construction market collapsed and even astute business-oriented contractors had to fight over table scraps. Those at the bottom of the food chain could no longer rely on the rising tide to sustain them and sank.

Let's not attribute too much to market dynamics, however. Long-lasting businesses prove themselves able to succeed through good times and bad. For the most part people who don't make a go at it running their own business succumb to mistakes made due to lack of business sense. Business sense is nothing more than common sense with a lot of money at stake.

A lot of mythology has been published about business failure rates. One that has made the rounds is that 50% fail in the first year and 95% go under within five years. Reliable data is hard to come by, and while failure rates vary among different types of businesses, failures don't appear to be that high overall. A 2005 study by the Small Business Administration (SBA) calculates that about two-thirds of new business establishments survive at least two years and 51% are still around after five years.

That sounds pretty good, although keep in mind that the SBA's definition of a "small business" encompasses firms with sales volume up to $50 million a year. Most so-called "mom and pop" start-ups would find even a tenth of those revenues the fulfillment of their wildest dreams. I suspect the failure rate is much higher for enterprises at the lowest end of SBA's scale.

Moreover, a quality of life issue needs to be addressed among small business owners. Between the heights of success and abject failure lay the teeming masses of businesses that carry on like D students hoping to someday graduate. Many small businesses hang around TOO long, in my opinion. Their owners struggle and continue to throw good money after bad when they have marketable skills they could parlay into comfortable incomes working for someone else.

Demand for their goods or services are sufficient and competition inept enough to keep them above the tipping point, often for a long time. Yet these businesses wallow in mediocrity. Owners and employees make a living but never quite claw their way to even the bottom rungs of affluence. Mediocre businesses can thrive when the economy is booming and the high tide raises all boats. Many capsized amid the low tide that swept in after our nation's quarter-century long construction boom.

Writing about business successes and failures is how I made my living, but even more instructive has been living itself. My professional life spanned only a little more than half of the years I've been on earth. My entire life has been devoted to something else.

That is consuming goods and services provided by businesses large and small. Most of the money I've ever earned has been spent helping to generate paychecks for business owners and their employees. That's life as we know it in a free enterprise economy, and I wouldn't have it any other way.

To a perceptive consumer, a lifetime of consumption is the equivalent of a Harvard MBA in recognizing when a business is doing something right or wrong. Like parenting, consuming is something that comes naturally. Just like parents, consumers learn from trial and error along the way. That's one reason why even lousy businesses can hang on for a while. It takes time for consumers to see the errors of their spending ways. They'll continue to patronize inferior businesses because of convenient location, force of habit, or they simply don't know of better alternatives. Over time, however, most consumers wise up. They figure out the best places to spend their money and favor those businesses over the ones lacking in smart business practices.

Most business owners and managers are reasonably smart people. Many of those I know have college degrees, usually in a business-related curriculum, and quite a few have gone on to acquire MBAs. Others are entrepreneurial types perhaps with clipped formal education but a lot of street smarts. A rather high amount of intelligence is required to keep track of all the details necessary to administer any business – dealing with suppliers, customer care, employee management, government regulations, finance, marketing and so on. You won't find too many genuinely stupid people running businesses.

What you will find is all those smart people making avoidable mistakes, over and over. Perceptive consumers almost daily experience head-smacking moments that cause them to seek out alternative places to patronize. More often than not, the alternatives sooner or later lead to similar bruises on the forehead.

Why do all those smart businesspeople continuously make mistakes? A big reason is that most business owners and managers are not very introspective about what they do. They are doers rather than thinkers. Running a business is time consuming. There are only so many hours to the day, and the thinking of most businesspeople tends to focus on the nuts and bolts of daily operations.

I'll draw an analogy from my line of work as a magazine editor for more than three decades. Editors constantly seek to eliminate typographical errors – mistakes in spelling, grammar, capitalization, punctuation and so on. It made me cringe every time I saw one in print that had slipped through all of our proofreading firewalls. Worst of all was when a typo would show up in a headline. Too many of these slipped through our defenses over the years. That's because proofreaders tend to focus so intently on the finer points of spelling, grammar, capitalization, punctuation in the main text that it's easy to overlook the glaring mistakes in big type screaming at them.

This book is intended to help you identify your headline errors and correct them before they damage your business irreparably.

Chapter 1—Business Basics

My Friend Ray

Ray had quit his job as a factory foreman a year or so before in order to go into business for himself. Landscaping was his calling, but in our part of the country that's seasonal work spanning half the year. Ray figured he'd fill in by painting the rest of the time.

There were family ties between my wife, Jenny, and Ray's wife. We had heard he was struggling in his new career and, with several rooms inside our house in need of painting, Jenny and I decided to throw some work his way. We didn't even talk price before hiring him. We trusted him to do right by us.

One day Ray was still finishing up when I arrived home from work. He pointed apologetically to a receipt left on our dining room table for paint he had bought, for which he took no markup. His tone suggested a sense of guilt in charging us for the paint. That made me strike up a conversation about his business. I learned the following.

Ray was going to charge me his standard rate of $35 an hour, which he said was what most painters in our area were charging. (This was back in the early 1990s, but even then it was rather cheap.) That's what I'd likely pay if I had hired one of the big companies advertising in the Yellow Pages, he said. He pointed out that the going rate was about the same in the landscaping side of his business. Most landscaping contractors used undocumented immigrant workers and paid them around $8 an hour with zilch benefits. He felt that if he charged more he'd never be able to get enough work.

During summer months his teenage son worked with him. His son's pay came out of the $35 an hour he charged customers. Ray lived about 50 miles away, yet he did not intend to charge us any more than his standard labor rate, even though his battered pickup truck slurped about a third of a tank of gas with each round trip.

Ray had been making $52,000 a year as a factory foreman with good benefits, he confided. He thought he would make more than that working for himself, but the business wasn't going as well as he expected. Didn't have enough customers, was the way he saw the problem.

I liked Ray. That's why I walked him through some basic arithmetic of a trade contracting business.

Arithmetic doesn't lie

Suppose, Ray, you had all the work you could handle, I said. Suppose you were booked eight hours a day, five days a week, 50 weeks a year, allowing two weeks for vacation. That projects to 2,000 billable hours a year. Multiply that by $35 and it equals $70,000 in annual revenue for your little business. Out of that you pay your son for his labor, plus all overhead. Oh, and don't forget to include the cost of the benefits you walked away from when employed at the factory.

No matter how lean you operate, I told him, there's no way your overhead is going to run much less than 20% of your revenues. Now do the math. The only way to improve on his former factory job while charging $35 an hour would be to put steep markups on paint and materials, although Ray assured me that's just not done in either landscaping or house painting.

But wait, Ray, your situation is even bleaker. Much bleaker. That's because you don't have a prayer of booking 2,000 billable hours in a year. You'll be lucky to get 1,000 billable hours, and that's only if you spend half your waking hours hustling up work. That projects to $35,000 a year in revenues, minus your son's pay and overhead. Are you beginning to understand why you're having trouble making ends meet, Ray?

Stinkin' thinkin'

Ray was a pretty smart guy in most ways, as evidenced by rising to a supervisory position in his previous job. Yet the look on his face told me he had never figured this arithmetic before staking out on his own.

7

In general, I would say that the less money you have to borrow to start a business, the better off you are. In this case, though, Ray would've been better off going to a bank for startup money rather than tapping his own meager savings. That's because a banker would have asked to see a business plan, one that would incorporate some of the basic business arithmetic that I pointed out to him.

Rays exist in every business, but especially in the construction trades. Most trade workers strike out on their own with little more than a vague idea of the economics of their business. All they know is what they are "supposed" to charge based on the going rate their area. Then they cross their fingers hoping it will generate enough income to pay their bills and then some.

Let's analyze this stinkin' thinkin' one step at a time.

- **The "going rate" is sacred.**

Ray didn't dare charge more than what most others in the business charged. He admitted competitors got away with it by exploiting illegal immigrant labor, but he didn't follow the train of logic to understand that he couldn't possibly compete against that. He was afraid to charge more than the going rate because he might not get enough work, but even with competitive rates his business was on the verge of collapse because he wasn't getting enough work. That's because he lacked marketing savvy. He was relying entirely on word of mouth to recruit customers. That might work if he was a social butterfly with hundreds of close friends and business associates, but Ray was a rather shy guy without a large social circle.

- **How come others get away with it?**

Even after I pointed out the stark arithmetic of his situation, Ray still wasn't quite convinced. "How do all those other painters get away with charging $35 an hour?" he asked. Part of the answer was that many were undergoing the same struggles he was and would eventually go out of business. If you have a decent line of credit, you can lose money for a long time but stay afloat thanks to lenders who make their own big mistake of throwing good money after bad.

Those that were succeeding were doing so on the backs of those $8-dollar-an-hour laborers. Given enough volume, economies of scale would kick in and the remaining $27 an hour the contractors charged might be enough to cover overhead and provide significant profit dollars for the owners. Some of those companies probably were billing hundreds of hours per day via multiple work crews and benefitting from service contracts and repeat business unavailable to start-ups.

- **Overhead is trivial**.

When the average consumer hears that a business charges $35 an hour, s/he tends to think in terms of wages, which would be pretty good money. Non-businesspeople may know vaguely that there's some overhead involved, but they don't dive into the arithmetic. Surveys have shown that non-businesspeople think that businesses keep the overwhelming majority of their sales volume as profit, as opposed to the measly sub-10% range that characterizes most businesses. Many new business owners think the same way before they come in for their rude awakening.

Some types of businesses, mainly those centered around specialized knowledge, can get by with relatively little overhead. Business consultants, freelance writers, financial/tax advisors and so on often work out of a home office and need little more than a desk, telephone and computer to function. Yet I've found that even these knowledge workers tend to underestimate the amount of expenses entailed in peddling their intellectual wares. Office supplies and equipment, transportation and travel, marketing costs and so on tend to creep up faster than billing rates for such services.

- **It's somehow unethical to charge extra for materials.**

Ray didn't bill me for the time he spent going to the paint store, or for the cash flow deficit he suffered by paying out of pocket. Pickup and delivery of materials is a value-added function that entitles the provider to a markup. If customers want to save a few bucks, give them the option to pick up and haul the goods from a supplier, but most have better things to do with their time. What exactly is wrong with charging customers more for materials you go to the trouble of providing?

- **Business and friendship often clash.**

Even though he faced a 100-mile daily round trip to do my job, Ray refused to charge me more than his pitiful standard labor rate. In his mind, he was giving me a "family" discount. I've seen this behavior in a lot of trade contractors. They are nice guys who will eat various expenses for relatives, friends, neighbors, churches, friends of friends and so on. Of course, when you start a small business a large portion of your business at the beginning is likely to come via word of mouth from relatives, friends, neighbors, churches, friends of friends and so on. So, in essence these favors amount to a lowering of already inadequate standard prices.

- **Price is paramount.**

Yes, that's all many people are interested in. Low bidder gets the job, end of story. But not everyone is like that. I wasn't looking for the lowest possible price when I hired Ray. I was looking for someone who would do a good job painting my house with a minimum of hassles for me. Many customers are less interested in the price of a job than in the results.

Business owners who know how to market themselves can seek out these people and sell themselves on the basis of quality and innovation rather than price. Unfortunately, the vast majority of business owners know nothing about marketing except buying business with the lowest price or one pegged to a suicidal "going rate."

Calling it quits

A few weeks after finishing my job, Ray and his wife came to our house for dinner. Ray asked me to explain to her the same things I'd told him. I ran through the numbers again and opined that Ray would have to at least triple his labor rate in order to make a decent living, or put hefty markups on the paint and plants he provided to customers, or do some combination of labor and material increases. Or, mimic the big contractors and hire dirt cheap labor to do the work while concentrating on marketing the business. Ray had neither the will nor skill to do these things, though.

Ray and his wife had trouble believing he couldn't make a go of it simply by doing good work at prices people were used to paying. Yet, try as they might they couldn't find any loopholes in the stark arithmetic. They moved out of town a few months later to pursue a different dream in a distant state. They struggled mightily for a couple of years until finding steady jobs at decent pay.

Should I feel guilty about having extinguished someone's entrepreneurial fire? Or should I get a pat on the back?

I told this story to my good friend Ellen Rohr (www.barebonesbiz.com), who commented: "If he had the 'FIZZ,' he wouldn't be dissuaded. You need the fizz (i.e., entrepreneurial desire) in order to succeed in business."

Should You Go Into Business For Yourself?

This leads us to the premier, most fundamental business mistake. That's when people who don't know a thing about what it takes to run a business decide to go into business for themselves.

Many employees get bitten by the entrepreneurial bug after they've worked in a field long enough to acquire the necessary expertise. This notion runs especially rampant among construction trade workers, because of low barriers to entry for becoming a construction or service trade contractor.

Independent contractors don't even need an office or shop. They can work out of their home and haul everything they need to do the work in an old pickup truck, and that indeed is how many start out. Materials can be purchased on credit and paid for after they get paid for the work performed. The main requirement, or so they think, is their ability to work with the tools of their trade, and many are supremely talented in that regard. That's why at some point virtually all construction trade workers think about going into business for themselves.

Usually they're motivated by a desire to make more money or to be their own boss. All too often it happens when they feel they're not being treated right by their employer.

This is an incredibly important decision, and a very personal one. I wouldn't presume to tell you whether or not to go into business for yourself — no more than I would try to tell you who to marry or what to name your kids.

What I am willing to do is to lay out the pros and cons involved in running one's own business, to help readers so inclined make an informed decision about it.

Money talks

First, let's deal with the pro side of the ledger. What are the positive things that can happen if you decide to break out on your own?

Most obvious is the opportunity to make a lot more money. No matter how good you are at what you do, and no matter how successful the company you work for might be, there is a limit to how much any employer is willing to pay most workers. For many small businesses, the economics make it difficult for anyone except the owner to be pulling down a six-figure salary. This can be frustrating if you're a star performer working for a small company that shows no sign of getting much bigger.

Many small business owners do bring home incomes ranging well into six figures, along with various perks. The sky's the limit when you operate a profitable, growing business.

In addition to paying themselves a handsome salary, owners who build a successful business may someday find that other people want to buy it. If the company is successful enough, it could be worth millions of dollars in the owner's pocket, plus the owner often gets kept on the payroll as a highly paid manager or consultant. This is a payoff worth striving for. Furthermore, business owners enjoy tax deductions that also benefit them personally, such as a company car, entertainment write-offs, meals in fancy restaurants, country club dues and so on.

When you get right down to it, there are only a handful of ways to get rich. One is to inherit wealth. Another is to get extremely lucky winning a lottery, beating the casino or guessing right with the stock market. If you are a world-class athlete or entertainer, that also could be the path to crazy affluence.

For most people these methods are unattainable. If you're not born right or don't get wealth bestowed on you through sheer dumb luck, the most accessible path to getting rich is to own your own business.

It's good to be boss

Next to money, people get motivated to start their own business by a desire to be their own boss. Some people just don't like to answer to anyone else. If you're the kind of person who doesn't react well to authority, maybe you ought to seriously consider being your own boss.

Another extremely good reason to start one's own company is entrepreneurial drive. An entrepreneur is the business world's version of an artist. The true entrepreneur is a creative person who desperately needs an outlet to implement his or her ideas.

Being an entrepreneur differs from simply wanting to be your own boss. Many people want to be their own boss for negative reasons, because they feel underpaid or don't like the folks they work for.

With entrepreneurs, the desire to break away is present even if they like their job and their employer. They are like artists craving paint and a canvas, or musicians who would hock just about all of their possessions for an instrument. The entrepreneur has a creative vision about how to run a business, and that's what drives this person. If you fit the entrepreneurial mold, then the decision to start your own business is already made. Nothing can stop you.

Being an entrepreneur doesn't mean you'll automatically succeed. Many entrepreneurs fail in their business ventures, often several times.

In fact, there are some aspects of an entrepreneurial personality that go against the grain of what it takes to succeed in business over the long run. Too often the entrepreneur is a control freak who doesn't know how to delegate. S/he may be headstrong with a "my way or the highway" attitude.

These are not good qualities for running a successful business. Business success requires people skills, negotiating skills and willingness to compromise. It's not unusual for an entrepreneur to start out strong because of the brilliance of his or her business ideas, but then the flame fizzles out because of an inability to work with others.

But even when s/he fails, a true entrepreneur will continue to find a way to open up a new business again, sometimes in an entirely different field. If you are an entrepreneur, deep down, you probably know it. And you probably have always intended to start your own business from the minute you went to work for someone else.

Other motives

Another positive aspect of running your own business is the opportunity to do it right — or at least what you may perceive to be the right way. Some people disagree with the business practices of their employers. It can get frustrating seeing people above you make mistakes, but they won't listen to you because, after all, they're the boss. In some companies, opening your mouth will only get you in trouble. Owning your own business gives you a chance to do things the way you think they should be done and implement your ideas.

Job security is another reason why some people go into business for themselves. Construction trade workers in particular get tired of being laid off or not knowing how many hours they'll get from week to week. They think the only way they can assure themselves of employment is to be the one generating the work. Money often is secondary to such people. I've known trade contractors who earn less money than their top employees, but they're satisfied just knowing that nobody can fire them.

In fact, it's common for construction contractors to go into business for themselves after being laid off or fired. These people don't necessarily want to run their own business. The decision gets forced on them by necessity. Usually they are not very successful.

Finally, let's face it, a lot of prestige and ego gratification come with owning your own company. If you wish, you can name the company after yourself and put your name on vehicles and advertisements that get seen all over town. Most people would deny this as a motive, but deep inside I think most business owners get a kick out of being a big shot.

This pretty much covers the pro side of the ledger. The advantages of running your own business can be summarized as follows:

- The opportunity to earn big money.
- Satisfying the entrepreneurial urge.
- Opportunity to operate the way you think a business should.
- Job security.
- Prestige and ego gratification.

Now let's take a look at some of the biggest reasons to think twice about starting your own business.

Now for the bad news (and there's plenty of it)

If you're a sports fan, you may have noticed that great athletes seldom make the best coaches. Someone blessed with superior athletic ability typically has trouble understanding and motivating players with lesser skills. Great athletes succeed through raw talent brought to peak performance via hard work. Coaches need people skills and organizational ability. It's rare to find all of those ingredients in one package.

The same holds true for first-rate employees in any walk of life. Being a great craft worker, salesperson, accountant, etc., does not automatically translate to management success. The skills required to run a business are only marginally related to operational job skills. Businesses almost never fail because the owner lacks sufficient knowledge of a field or technical ability to do the work. Superior technical skills are what motivate them to get going on their own. When they fail it's usually because of a lack of good business sense, which leads to mistakes.

The keys to success in business lay in three areas:

1. Money;
2. Marketing;
3. People skills.

You have to be a good money manager and good people manager, and a promoter. If none of this sounds appealing to you, better think twice about starting your own business.

M-O-N-E-Y

Earlier I identified money as the main reason most people go into business for themselves. I stated that owning a business offers the possibility of getting rich and that many business owners make six-figure incomes. However, they are not the majority. A harsh fact of life is that more business owners go broke than get rich, and many spend a lifetime running businesses that struggle to get by.

If succeeding in business were easy, everyone would start his own company. What stops most people is the risk involved. The potential of big rewards entails comparable big risk. The larger and more ambitious your business vision, the more you'll have to lose.

As an employee, if you lose your job the worst thing that's likely to happen is you'll be unemployed for a period of time and lose income during that period. When a business fails, not only does the owner lose an income, s/he will be out all the money invested in the business, plus all that may be owed to creditors. It might be your own savings that go down the drain, or it may be money borrowed from a bank or from friends or relatives. In any case, it's not a good feeling to wonder how you're going to put food on the table PLUS pay back what you owe.

Even if the business doesn't go bankrupt, many stay solvent for a long time but barely get by and their owners scrape by on minimal incomes. Many business owners end up earning less than they could working for someone else.

Overhead headaches

The main reason for this is that many people who go into business for themselves don't have a clue about business economics. For instance, a trade worker's eyes get big seeing the difference between what s/he is making and what the company charges for that worker's labor. A skilled trade worker might be getting paid $15-20 an hour, and notices that the company bills customers for labor at $75-$100 an hour or even more. S/he starts to think, *I could make four or five times as much working for myself!*

This stinkin' thinkin' fails to account for overhead. Overhead structure varies greatly depending on the type of business. In the construction trades arena overhead typically will range from 20% to 40% of revenues or even higher. A lot of people entering the business think they can cut costs to the bone by working out of their homes and scraping by with old tools and equipment. Yet even doing that, there are certain large expenses that can't be cut very much.

For instance, let's take the most essential large expense, vehicles and equipment. A lot of trade contractors start out with beat-up trucks and rigs. But the more beat up, the more money they have to sink into maintenance and repairs. And what happens when the equipment breaks down and they can't make it to jobs? They lose not only money but also credibility with customers. That's no way to run a business.

In a merchandising business, the major expense is likely to be the cost of goods sold. You need inventory to sell and financing that inventory eats up a lot of money. Considerable risk is involved. Buy too much merchandise and you'll get stuck with a bunch of stuff if you don't sell as much as anticipated. Invest too little and you won't be able to meet customers' needs, which will send them scurrying to competitors.

Insurance, tools, advertising and so on cost more than most new business owners imagine going in. The suppliers of those things must be paid if you are going to stay in business. So, when money gets tight, the most convenient expense to cut is the owner's income. That's why for every business owner making a hundred grand a year, there are dozens struggling to make ends meet.

The office slave

Another trap many fledgling business owners fall victim to involves the spouse working in the business at little or no salary. Typically, hubby heads up operations while the wife serves as bookkeeper and office manager. They think of themselves as a team, and they figure this is a great way to keep costs down instead of hiring someone to do the office work.

Think hard about this for a moment. Would you really come out ahead?

Your spouse's services may seem free, but it's an illusion. If your wife is smart enough to run the family business, she's smart enough to earn a salary managing someone else's office. So even if she's not getting paid, you ought to factor into overhead what's known as an opportunity cost. The time she spends keeping the family business books for free is time she could be out earning money working for someone else. Her "free" services may be costing your family tens of thousands of dollars a year -- whatever she could command in the open market as a bookkeeper for some other firm.

Grueling hours

Another downside to running your own business is the hours you must put in. It's never a 40-hour-a-week job, and the first few years after start-up are the most grueling of all. Expect to put in 60 hours a week minimum, and don't be surprised if it escalates to 70- and even 80-hour weeks during peak periods or when problems develop. Don't expect to take many days off, and forget about lengthy vacations.

If you have children, as a start-up business owner you better resign yourself to the fact that you are going to miss out on school plays, ball games and other events that are part of growing up — and once missed can never be made up. When you're starting out in business, it's very difficult to take personal time off. Customers and business emergencies have a way of trumping family needs.

Many of the hours you work are going to be unbillable time. You'll be working 12-hour days and more, but for only a fraction of that time will you be generating income. The rest of the time will be spent trying to drum up customers, dealing with suppliers and so on.

Let's be optimistic and say that during the first year in business, an owner earns $50,000 in income before taxes and deductions. This is a realistic number. It's not exactly getting rich, but it's enough for most people to survive on.

What will it take to generate that income? Starting out most business owners would almost certainly have to put in at least 3,000 hours of work in a year. This is a realistic number, even a bit on the conservative side. It averages out to 50 weeks at 60 hours a week.

Now divide that $50,000 income by 3,000 hours. It comes to an hourly wage of about $16.67 an hour. How does this compare with what your marketable skills can command as someone else's employee?

If you have a spouse working in the business for free, you need to add her/his hours into the equation. Let's say s/he's only needed part-time to keep the books, say 1,000 hours a year. Now divide that $50,000 by 4,000 hours. As a couple, you would be working for an average of $12.50 an hour. If the spouse regularly puts in 40-hour weeks, divide that $50,000 by 5,000 hours, or $10.00 an hour. The two of you can make that much slinging burgers in a fast-food joint.

This just addresses income. People who are self-employed also need to provide health insurance for themselves, and ideally some kind of retirement savings plan.

And what happens if you come down with the flu? Who is going to run the business? I've seen self-employed trade workers force themselves to work when they're so sick they can hardly walk. Serious illness is unthinkable. You better have terrific disability or worker's comp insurance. However, the sad truth is that most novice business owners are uninsured or underinsured.

Of course, once a business becomes established and successful, the owners don't have to work so hard. Employees may see their bosses taking afternoons off to play golf and maybe disappear for several weeks a year on exotic vacations. That's the reward for operating a successful business. Just keep in mind that most of those people spent many years working 3,000 hours and more at pitiful incomes to build their business to the point where they can take it easy.

Small vs. big

Many businesses start out as a one-person operation, maybe with the spouse pitching in as just discussed. At most, you may have a partner and perhaps an employee or two. Few new business owners can afford to support a large staff right from the start. That's why you can expect to put in so many hours. You may think that one of the attractions of owning your own business is the opportunity to work at your own pace and take time off when you feel like it. The reality for most small business owners is that survival means spending almost every waking hour on the job, and even when "relaxing" at home you'll spend a lot of time thinking about and working on business issues.

Still, many business owners choose to remain small, believing it leads to fewer headaches. This is a personal decision and not necessarily a bad one depending on your goals and your values. Business is indeed less complicated when you have only yourself to manage. But keep in mind that staying small also has its drawbacks.

The biggest is simply that it limits your income potential. For instance, a rough rule of thumb for small shops is that the owner can expect to take home about 10% of billings as personal compensation. So, to make $50,000 a year, you need to generate around $500,000 in annual revenues.

How realistic is that? It comes out to almost $42,000 a month, which translates to a little under $10,000 a week, or a little under $2,000 a day, every working day.

How many of you have the capability of booking that much work or selling that much merchandise? Even if you could pull it off, it virtually guarantees 60- and 70-hour work weeks when you factor in paperwork, marketing and other administrative tasks.

And this is just to earn 50 Gs. If your goal is that six-figure milestone, double the arithmetic. For a business in a competitive field, that's very hard to achieve as a one-person operation.

Like all rules of thumb, the 10% rule is not carved in stone. Some small business owners put more than 10% of billings in their pocket, and as companies grow larger the percentage taken by the owner tends to decrease. For example, you won't find many owners of a $10 million business compensating themselves to the tune of $1 million a year. As businesses grow larger, additional overhead tends to gobble up money and funds are needed to finance expansion. Nonetheless, if making big bucks is your goal, it virtually demands that you grow your business to a decent size.

Growth means hiring other people to work for you. Finding good people is perhaps the most difficult part of running a business.

Managing people

By "good" I don't mean just in job skills. Small businesses require employees who are trustworthy, reliable and capable of doing their jobs effectively with minimal supervision. People who might thrive within a large corporate structure are not necessarily a good fit to work in a small business, and vice versa.

Even if you manage to find good employees, keeping them happy and motivated is not easy. Managing people is an art. Big corporations devote many hours of training before they put someone in charge of others. People in a small company seldom get any management training at all. They simply get told to supervise other people. Being bossed around by incompetent supervisors is a big reason why so many underlings think about starting their own business.

Then the cycle perpetuates itself. Employees who get treated like dirt become business owners and treat their people the same way, because that's the only way they know how to manage. Yet if you want to grow your business, success will depend not on you alone, but on the people you hire. Somehow you must motivate them to peak performance.

Maybe you have that ability. Some people are natural born leaders who know how to motivate people as if by instinct. Do some soul searching and ask yourself if you really are one of them. Have you ascended to leadership positions throughout your life in school, athletics or other endeavors? If the honest answer is yes, then it's a good bet you have the leadership skills needed to succeed in business.

Just be mindful that society has far more followers than leaders – and most appointed leaders are there by default rather than ability. Just as great athletes don't necessarily make the best coaches, there is not a shred of correlation between technical skills and leadership ability. There might even be a slight negative correlation, because people with superior technical skills tend to be at their best when working alone to concentrate on tasks at hand without distractions from others around them.

Legal issues

Laws and government regulations present another formidable obstacle for those who would run their own business. Business owners often spend more time filling out government paperwork than they do managing their businesses. Every government agency from OSHA to EPA to EEOC to DOE to DOT has its tentacles in small businesses. Big corporations can afford to hire specialized staff to deal with all their issues. Mom and pop businesses have to somehow maneuver around all the curves by themselves.

Also, all business owners live under the constant threat of lawsuits, often for things beyond their control. Lawsuits can get filed by suppliers who don't get paid, by workers who get hurt on the job, by employees who feel they've been mistreated, by customers who think they got a raw deal. Sooner or later most businesses get caught up in litigation of some kind, and if you want to see how fast money can get sucked into a black hole, just wait until you start dealing with lawyers on a regular basis.

Summary

Just as we did with the plus side, let's summarize the downsides of owning your own business:

• You probably won't make as much money as you think you will, especially from the start.

• You risk the money you've invested and maybe borrowed to start your business.

• You are guaranteed to work long hours.

• As a one-person operator, you need to provide some sort of backup plan in case you get sick or want to take some time off.

• If you are not a one-person operator, you have the headaches of hiring and managing other people — and the unpleasant duty of firing some along the way.

• You will spend a disproportionate amount of time dealing with legal matters and government regulations.

Are you sure you still want to be your own boss?

Maybe I've just painted an overly bleak picture of business ownership. I'm simply trying to point out that it's important for budding entrepreneurs to go into such an important venture with your eyes fully open. What it boils down to is risk and hard work on one side of the equation, balanced by rewards on the other. Risk and rewards go hand in hand with business ownership. You can't have one without the other.

But also keep in mind that millions of small business owners across the country manage to overcome all the obstacles and thrive. A few become wealthy beyond their wildest dreams. It's been proven countless times that no obstacles are too big to overcome with sufficient talent and drive.

A Dozen Business Basics

Suppose your decision is made. You are going to take a fling at owning a business, or maybe you already own one. Everyone who runs a business ought to know keep in mind the following 12 basic business concepts.

1. Business skills are different than technical skills.
Bill Gates started out as a brilliant computer programmer, but as

time passed he didn't spend any time writing code for Microsoft. Don't ask Ben & Jerry to make you a sundae, or Mrs. Field to bake you some cookies. Thomas Edison died a wealthy man not so much because of his revolutionary inventions, but because he got out of the laboratory and proved astute at marketing his discoveries. Giant electric utilities now known as ComEd and Con Ed are among the businesses that arose from original Edison ventures.

The lessons are everywhere you care to look. You may know everything there is to know about widgets, but that's quite different than knowing how to run a successful widget business.

Running a business requires financial, sales, marketing, negotiating, supervisory, leadership and customer service skills. The business world is filled with technically astute workers who can work magic with the tools of their trade, but who do not understand the costs of doing business and how to market their firms in any way except via the lowest price. They approach business as a way to buy themselves a job rather than a profit-generating enterprise.

If you're thinking of opening a business of your own, please do yourself and everyone else in your field a favor by delaying your startup until you've taken enough business courses or seminars to understand what needs to be done to operate profitably. Don't define success solely by the amount of work you get or sales revenue generated. The purpose of business is not to make sales, but to make money. If you lose money on everything you do, it's guaranteed you won't make it up in volume! If you don't manage your costs and sell your goods, services and know-how at the prices needed to be profitable, you are better off remaining someone else's employee.

2. You need both salary and profits.

Many small business owners mistakenly believe that profit equates with income. That is, whatever is left of their revenues after all bills get paid is what they live off. If there are no profits, they make do as best they can by tapping savings, borrowing money and delaying payment to creditors. This is an expressway to bankruptcy.

Studies have shown that it takes an average of three years for a new business to turn a profit. This means anyone starting a business needs to have enough funding not only to pay business expenses but also to support their families through the initial money-losing years.

(Ellen Rohr doesn't buy the notion that a new business can expect to lose money for a long time. Her bootstrapping clients get told, "Make money EVERY MONTH!" Ellen understands that might prove impossible in the real world, but it's a great goal to strive for and will likely result in a laser-like focus on keeping revenues up and expenses down.)

As the owner of a privately-held business, you need to budget a salary draw for yourself, and build that draw into the selling price of goods and services. You may need to take home a modest salary when first starting out, but at least make sure you can pay the mortgage and put food on the table.

3. Charge enough to make money.

Different businesses have different profit structures. Grocery chains and other high-volume merchandising businesses with rapid inventory turnover often can succeed with net profit margins in the range of 1%. Manufacturing and other capital-intensive businesses demand double-digit bottom lines. Whatever the case may be for your particular business, be sure to factor in profit margins large enough to cover essential living expenses.

But if I did that, my prices won't be competitive!

Many struggling business owners have said that to me. Like my friend, Ray, they can't make it on the prices they charge but worry that raising them will turn customers away. They await a boost in profit dollars from increased sales volume but that can be a long wait. Without more sales either they have to raise their prices or lower their costs, or some combination of both, to turn the situation around. Many do little more than cross their fingers and hope for the same kind of divine intervention that is said to have turned water into wine, only in this case turn dimes into dollars.

A similar response I've heard from time to time is:

My competitors charge the same prices and they make it. Why can't I?

My response to that one has always been twofold: 1. Are you sure your competitors are really making it? 2. If they are, maybe it's because they have a different cost structure or other economies not apparent at a glance. For instance, maybe they operate out of a building they own that's paid up, while you are burdened with a hefty mortgage or lease. Maybe they've got access to "sugar daddy" family or friend financing. For all you know, maybe their business is structured to lose money as part of a larger enterprise looking for tax deductions or to launder money.

Small business owners have a way of deluding themselves into thinking that just because competitors do things a certain way, that's the way to do it. In particular, they think the "going rate" for the products and services they sell in a particular market is the price they must sell at.

The "going rate" is a quicksand pit for many small businesses. In most cases the going rate is synonymous with the lowest prices around. Some businesses are structured to be successful with lowball pricing – think Wal-Mart. Typically, these are large, well-established and sophisticated businesses with the clout to squeeze suppliers and realize massive operational economies of scale.

A lot of people resent Wal-Mart because they tend to drive locally owned retailers out of business. Upon closer inspection I think you'll find that only the weakest businesses fall victim. Look in the vicinity of any Wal-Mart store and you'll likely find scores of small shops selling the same kinds of merchandise you can find in Wal-Mart. Mom and pop competitors draw their share of customers because they offer things shoppers won't find at the giant store, be it different brands, personalized service, friendly atmosphere and so on. Also keep in mind that the small business isn't competing against Wal-Mart for every single customer. Wal-Mart needs thousands of people coming through the doors every day. The Mom-'n-Pops just need to pick off a few of them to be successful.

More troublesome than large corporate competitors is that the going rate for a particular kind of business more often gets established not by the Wal-Marts of the world, but by fellow small business owners who don't have a clue what they're doing and are headed toward bankruptcy. As a budding business owner, you can be a lemming following them off a cliff – or else you need to figure out a way to market yourself on something other than price. Otherwise you will work too hard for too little money, and stay perpetually squeezed for as long as you stay in business.

4. The customer is NOT always right, but you better pretend.

That old saying about the customer always being right is not literally true. Often you'll find customers to be unreasonable, cantankerous and a royal pain in the anatomy. But that's a reality you need to suppress for success in business.

A better mindset is to try your best to do everything possible to satisfy every customer. Sometimes that will prove impossible. Sometimes the customer will be unrealistic in his demands. Sometimes you may even determine you would be better off "firing" a given customer. But before you reach these conclusions, give the customer some benefit of the doubt. Pretend that s/he's right and you're wrong. Do your best to give in to what the customer wants, and force yourself to be cheerful when doing it. You'll find out that, more often than not, this behavior pays off.

Keep in mind that you can never win an argument with a customer. Even if you "win" by being proven right, the outcome will most likely be that the customer will walk away angry and you will lose that business forever. Is that what you'd call victory?

5. It's not what you say, it's how you say it.

At some point you've probably gone into a retail store and seen one of those signs that reads: "Absolutely no refunds after seven days"?

Friendlier stores have a sign that reads: "We will cheerfully refund any merchandise returned within seven days of purchase!"

Can you detect any difference in their return policies? Yet which store would you rather do business with?

6. Under-promise and over-deliver.

Most businesses do the exact opposite. They will say anything a customer wants to hear just to get the person off their back. "The job will take no more than two weeks ... Your order will be here in a couple of days ... We'll get that taken care of right away."

It's not that everyone purposely fibs. In most cases comments like that reflect best-case scenarios of what would happen if everything went right. It's just that in the real world, suppliers don't come through, workers call in sick, schedules and deliveries get botched because of weather or other events beyond your control, and so on.

Just remember this simple rule. If you promise something in a week and it takes 10 days, you're a bum. But if you promise something in two weeks and it takes 10 days, you're a hero.

7. Make it easy to do business with you.

Some companies act as if they are doing the customer a favor by agreeing to supply them with the goods or services they need. Everything must be scheduled at the business's convenience rather than the customer's. Phone calls get returned when the spirit moves them. Something seems to go wrong with every transaction.

Your business is nothing without your customers. A business owner must lavish attention on customers, not just tolerate them. If you have policies and procedures in place that make it difficult for them to deal with you, simplify those rules, remove those barriers.

8. Every business owner is a salesperson.

Many technically astute business owners, craftsmen in particular, think selling is beneath their dignity. They prefer to focus on the technical and operations side of their business and believe they can do things so well customers will simply flock to them without prodding. They believe in the old saying that if you build a better mousetrap the world will beat a path to your door.

Sorry, but that's the business world's version of a fairy tale. In virtually every business, you can look around and find numerous competitors who can do what you do just as well or better, and you can always find someone to do it at a lower price. Selling means convincing people you offer better value.

9. What's your USP?

Every business needs a Unique Selling Proposition (USP). That is, why should a customer do business with you as opposed to a competitor? Anyone opening a new business needs to ask that question and then build a marketing strategy around it.

There are three basic marketing strategies:

1. Low price.
2. Filling a niche.
3. Differentiation.

Little companies have a lot of trouble pursuing the first. Unfortunately, most small business owners don't know that. The only thing they know about marketing is that they'll get more business if their prices are cheaper than the competition's. But being in business isn't about obtaining volume. It's about making money. Think twice about trying to succeed on the basis of lowest price.

Filling a niche is simply applying the old baseball philosophy of "hit 'em where they ain't." If your business offers specialized services with little competition in a given market, that's a good head start toward business success. Restaurants have a notoriously high failure rate, a big reason being that they often spring from the owner's personal talents and tastes. You may make the best lasagna around, but if there are a dozen Italian restaurants in the area, you may be better off opening up in an area lacking Italian cuisine.

Differentiation means offering something a little different. Maybe you sell the same goods or services as other competitors but have a unique twist. Think of those specialty clothing stores that cater to "plus-size" customers who have a hard time finding clothes that fit from the major clothing retailers, or boutique stores that offer a wide selection of goods in a narrow category.

10. Selling and marketing are constant.

Success in business requires constant selling and marketing, even if you have more business than you can handle. Here's why:

A. If you have more business than you can handle, you want to focus on the most profitable segment of that business. Strive to get more business out of your most profitable customers while winnowing out those who don't want to pay enough or give you trouble.

B. Relying only on word-of-mouth is putting your fate in the hands of other people. It's dangerous to depend on anyone else to make you successful.

C. Sooner or later every business hits dry spells. When it does, you'll be desperate to start generating business, but it will take months for any marketing efforts to kick in. The best time to prepare for a slowdown is in advance of it occurring.

11. Successful businesses must continue to grow.

"Grow or die" is a famous maxim from Peter Drucker, one the smartest business management geniuses who ever lived. This doesn't mean every business has to grow big. Many of you don't want the headaches that come with getting big, and it's more important to be profitable than generate large revenues.

At the same time some amount of growth is necessary just for survival. Studies have shown that businesses lose an average of around 9% of their customers each year to natural attrition. People die, move away, or make new business friends, and you will lose those customers through absolutely no fault of your own. You have to continue to grow your business just to make up for those losses.

12. Successful business owners love their work.

I've never met a successful business owner, in any field, who didn't have a passion for the business. Running a business is hard work and filled with aggravation. If you don't love what you're doing, you'll get burned out quickly.

I've met too many business owners who always wear a frown and wallow in misery. They're the folks who are always griping about customers, competitors, suppliers, inspectors and so on. They find fault with everyone but themselves.

Many of them want nothing more than to be working with the tools of their trade, or making sales calls on customers, or fiddling with the numbers, or otherwise doing whatever it is they do best. They are in love with only a piece of their job as a business owner or manager.

Successful business owners must come to grips with all that it takes to run a successful business. Hardly any owner enjoys all aspects of the business, yet successful ones enjoy the challenge of figuring out ways to manage all the details whether that entails hands-on involvement, delegation or subbing out what they don't enjoy or can't do as well as someone else.

They love coming to work every day because they find the business stimulating and it brings them prosperity. There are few things in life more rewarding than making a good living doing what you love. If you can honestly say that you love going to work each day, then you've mastered a key to success in your business.

Character Counts

Please indulge me while I tell you of my proudest moment on the golf course. I promise not to bore you bragging of great shots or a low round. Quite the contrary, it concerns a lousy shot that may have cost me a tournament match.

My drive sliced right and headed perilously close to a wooded area marked by white out-of-bounds stakes — an all too familiar occurrence with my game. So, I hit a provisional ball that ended up where it belonged in the fairway, except it would represent my third shot. My opponent and two other playing partners all hit their drives to the left, so I trudged alone toward the woods to locate my first ball.

I found it lying close to a white stake. When I lined that marker up with an adjacent stake, the ball was unmistakably out of bounds. Not by more than a couple of feet, but only if you crossed your eyes would you judge it to be in play. My companions were almost 100 yards away and paying little attention to me. They couldn't possibly tell if I were in play or out of bounds.

I'm ashamed to say the thought flitted across my mind to save a shot by chipping out to the fairway, claiming the ball was in bounds. Prize money in addition to bragging rights were at stake, and match play always stirs my competitive juices. Daily doses of such temptation explain why there's an astounding amount of sin in our world.

But I turned my back on the devil. I took my penalty, played the provisional ball, and lost the hole by a stroke. The match was tight until I got closed out on the 17th hole. Had I cheated on that close out-of-bounds call, the outcome might have been different, although I'd have felt rotten inside.

Golf has a different ethic than most other sports. When a baseball player traps a ball, he instinctively raises his glove trying to fool the umpire into ruling he caught it on the fly. Basketball players are notorious for "flopping" in hopes of drawing a charging call. If a football player ever called a penalty on himself, he would catch hell from teammates, coaches and fans — and the referee would probably faint! Only golfers are expected to police themselves.

Most of the people I habitually golf with trust one another to do exactly that. My opponent left it entirely up to me to make the out-of-bounds call, and I would have done the same with him. This trust factor has bonded us into a harmonious golfing community, even though some of our personalities may clash off the course.

There are always exceptions. Years ago I played a match with an individual I noticed improving his lie when he thought no one was looking. I never called him on it, because there were no other witnesses and it would have led to an irresolvable "no I didn't ... yes you did" argument. However, the episode forged a lasting negative impression about that fellow. I've kept my distance from him and have never patronized the business he owns. I figure if he cheats at golf, he wouldn't hesitate to cheat his customers.

An epidemic of cheating

Some might call that harsh judgment. What does it matter if people take liberties with a silly pastime?

My response is that golf reveals more about people than their degree of skill with the clubs. Someone once defined morality as doing what's right when no one's watching. The golf course provides an ideal testing ground.

With that in mind, what are we to make of a survey commissioned in 2002 by the Starwood Hotels & Resorts chain? They queried 401 business executives and CEOs with an average household income of $187,000 on a variety of golf and related issues. Turns out that 82% of those executives admitted to cheating on the golf course. The survey also found 86% saying they cheated in business.

Sense a correlation there?

A similar study done in 1993 found only 55% of executives saying they cheated at golf – still too many but substantially lower than those found in the 2002 survey.

I don't know what happened in that nine-year interval to trigger so much more dishonesty in top business ranks, but it's probably not a coincidence that the early 2000s marked the start of a series of headline corporate fraud exposures with companies such as Enron, Adelphia, Qwest, WorldCom, Tyco, the list goes on and on. The Bernie Madoff affair was merely the crowning achievement of a long rogues gallery of top business leaders whose moral compass pointed south. In a bygone era it seemed only fair to assume the integrity of CEOs and CFOs until proven otherwise.

The Starwood survey suggests investors and the public at-large now do so at their risk. For a golf tournament to be worthwhile, scores must be accurate. For a market to be healthy, investors need to believe the numbers they get fed are legitimate. For that to happen, business executives and auditors need to recalibrate their moral compass.

A good start might be to drag themselves away from the bad company they keep at plush resorts and country clubs, and play a few rounds with me and my buddies at our municipal course.

Chapter 2—How Not To Make Money

Cash Flow Bottlenecks

Among the many hassles of uprooting one's residence is the need to establish new business relationships with all the people you rely on to keep up the household. I remember the time many years ago when Jenny and I moved into a new home and I asked a local acquaintance to recommend an electrical contractor to install some ceiling fans and light fixtures we had purchased for our new home.

This contractor almost lost my business before it began by waiting a couple of days to return my phone call. Big mistake. Small business owners should never be too busy to return calls from customers or prospects as promptly as possible. Find the time to do it, period. The call you miss could turn out to be a game changer for your business. Anyway, the owner finally got back to me just hours before I was about to renew my search for an electrician.

We arranged the work for May 21. The electrician who did the work turned out to be the owner's son. He was a personable young man in line to someday inherit the business. I was quite pleased with his performance. He showed up on time, worked efficiently, cleaned up afterward, and everything he installed worked just dandy. When he was done, I asked him if I could pay with a credit card, and he politely informed me they don't accept credit cards. I'd receive a bill in the mail.

On June 30, I finally received an invoice for his services. No complaint about this, either. His price turned out to be far less than I expected to pay. (Some of you might be scratching your heads wondering why with either Ray or the electrician I never asked ahead of time what I would be charged for their work. That's just a personal quirk when dealing with people I know and trust or get referred to by someone I trust. Had I felt I'd been gouged I would've dealt with the situation then – and put them on my black list -- but in all my encounters dealing with businesses through connections, that's never occurred.)

As a homeowner, I got a great deal. Yet, as one whose livelihood made me a soul mate of trade professionals, it was disheartening to experience yet another example of an honest, hard-working business owner making a big mistake.

This contractor left a satisfied customer in his wake, but took more than *five weeks*! to send a bill for his services, which he undersold by about half. He shunned credit cards no doubt because it galled him to pay the 2-3% vigorish charged by the issuer. In doing so he bypassed any interest he could've earned on money that would've gone into his account within days of the transaction, plus savings of paperwork and postage. The invoice didn't state any due date, and I bet if I were so inclined I could've gone months without paying before anyone bothered to call me to ask for the money. (Showing more respect for his business than the owner himself, I paid the bill a couple of days after receiving it.)

Credit cards are a great deal

Businesses that don't accept credit cards are making a big blunder. Anyone who operates a business where people can pay up front for goods and services ought to establish a merchant account and accept credit cards. Period. Don't give it a second thought. By all means shop around for the best deals. With enough research you'll likely find credit card issuers offering to take less than the 2-3% going rate that merchants typically get dinged, but even those modest fees are worthwhile considering all the advantages.

First and foremost, you get your money rapidly. Payments charged to credit cards normally get put into your account within a few days of the transaction. That money earns interest for you and shores up your cash flow. It saves additional money by reducing paperwork, postage and the labor associated with managing receivables, sending out invoices and processing payments.

Another big advantage of credit cards is that they eliminate one of the biggest headaches associated with running a business – collecting money owed.

If a customer doesn't pay his credit card bill, that's the credit card issuer's problem, not yours. You don't have to worry about checks bouncing or sending out nasty collection letters. Most businesses that extend credit tend to suffer 1-2% losses as uncollectable. Avoiding those losses by itself covers much of the credit card fees.

If you do extend credit to customers, at least send out your bills in timely fashion. Ideally, they should go out the same day as the transaction, or at least within 24 hours. It's customary to allow clients up to a month to pay before a bill is considered past due. Don't feel locked in by this standard practice, however. Instead of putting a due date on your invoice of 30 days beyond the transaction, have it say, "due upon receipt." Some customers will wait 30 days or more to pay anyway, but this will instill a sense of urgency in at least some people.

Various studies have shown that poor cash flow is as much a cause of business insolvency as lack of profits. That's because a business needs ample cash on hand to pay suppliers, creditors and employees – including the owner's personal living expenses. You may have more than enough locked up in receivables (money owed you) to pay your bills, but you won't hang on to good suppliers and good employees for very long if you keep delaying their payments.

It's astonishing why that electrical contractor would wait five weeks before sending a bill for his services. Businesses so lackadaisical about their money silently signal customers that they shouldn't be too concerned about rapid payment. Had I been in a tight money squeeze, this invoice would have topped my list of those to put off.

Invisible Overhead

I've seen the look more times than I can remember. Jaw slackens, brows wrinkle, eyes squint, hand scratches the back of their head. The business owner does two or three takes at the numbers before finally announcing, "They can't possibly do the job for that amount" ... or, "They can't possibly sell that product for that price and make any money."

The sad truth is that plenty of transactions get made for less money than it costs the owner to perform the work or provide the goods. There are many reasons for all the miscalculation, but here let's be content to draw attention to one of the most common causes of lowball selling prices.

Many small business owners don't have a complete handle on their overhead. They overlook stuff. Or, they know it's there but omit it because, well, if they included it their estimate might be too high to win the job or sale price too high to move the merchandise. Need to shave your bid? Simply ignore some overhead. Life is much simpler in this make-believe world. At least until the bills come due.

Let's take a tour of Business Never Land where certain expenses magically disappear at the brush of an eraser.

Modern slavery

One big mistake is something touched upon in Chapter 1, the widespread practice of small firms employing slave labor. I'm referring to the spouse that so many owners take on as a business partner without pay to keep the books and do other office functions. They're a team, you see, that's what marriage is all about. This free labor helps keep prices down to the point where the business can get more work than it can handle yet still not make any money.

The owner may think he's doing okay income-wise, except the income doesn't stack up so well when you consider it takes two people to earn it. Besides, it's an illusion that the spouse works for free. Opportunity cost comes into play. If she's smart enough to run your office, she's smart enough to go into the open market and do the same thing for pay running someone else's office. So even if you don't pay her, it's costing you money that she could be contributing to the household coffers if she were not occupied being your slave.

Abide by the Emancipation Proclamation and pay the wife or any other family member that does work for your business. Decide upon a reasonable salary for their services and build it into fixed overhead.

Bad enough they treat their spouses that way, some business owners themselves fail to take a salary draw. They practice "checkbook accounting," in which the owner keeps whatever is left over after the bills are paid. If there's nothing left — not an unusual occurrence — they typically stiff their suppliers, sometimes even their employees, in order to pay the mortgage and put food on the table. Meantime, they reduce prices to get some cash flowing. For some reason, this financial management technique never seems to work out too well for very long.

Depreciation & intangibles

Most business owners will include equipment depreciation in their tax returns, but many fail to account for it in their billing. Yet the fact remains that every mile you drive is one mile subtracted from the useful life of a company vehicle. Office equipment, computers and other devices also deteriorate and need to be replaced periodically. Where will the money come from? The answer in too many cases is out of the business owner's personal income, or maybe a kid's college fund.

Where it should be coming from are your customers. All of them benefit from the vehicles and equipment you use in running your business, and they all ought to pay a portion to replace the items that break or wear out. The fairest and simplest way to bill them is to factor into your overhead a depreciation expense to cover the inevitable need for replacements down the road.

Insurance is another big expense that business owners often fail to include in their selling prices. Again, they'll list it as a business expense for the IRS, but it's too hard to break down into an overhead amount, so they'll just skip it. Same with professional fees and dues, subscriptions, bad debts, legal and accounting fees, bank charges and other intangible items that don't have a fixed price tag every month like the electric and phone bills.

Speaking of which, even utility bills tend to get shortchanged by owners who do a significant amount of work out of their home. Although they usually have a separate business telephone, most tend to ignore the extra light, heat, water, a/c and other household expenses generated by their business activities. Also consider that if you work out of a basement or family room office, that is space not available for family use. This is another opportunity cost and there should be an overhead charge to cover it.

(Whether to include home office expense as a tax deduction is something you ought to discuss with a trusted tax advisor. Disadvantages, based on tax laws as of this writing, include the fact that it likely will lead to a larger tax bill if you sell your home, and increases your chance of an IRS tax audit.)

Consumables

Some business utilize an abundance of "cheap" consumables — everything from grease to fasteners to tape to paper towels to the six-packs of pop they may buy for their workers on a hot day. Taken individually the costs may amount to pocket change, but pocket change can add up to thousands of dollars a year.

Who pays for the gas your vehicles use making deliveries or otherwise going about business? What about the pens and paper, computer CDs, staples, grease markers, etc., that you use day after day? What about the office supplies used?

Your P & L – the key to tracking expenses

Every business owner needs to review a Profit & Loss Statement (P & L) at least monthly. Weekly or even daily P & L reports are even better. Small businesses that use outside accountants may have trouble getting their statements on a timely basis. This is something that should be negotiated before you hire an accounting firm. If you do your own accounting, various business software packages will enable you to print out P & Ls as often as you'd like.

A P & L is perhaps the most important document a business owner needs to track. It provides pictures, both panoramic and detailed, of business income and expenses. What follows is a plentiful but hardly exhaustive list of overhead line items you should track for your P & L statements AND for inclusion in your selling prices. The more line items you can break out, the better will be your handle on business expenses.

- Salary — Owner(s)
- Salaries — Supervisors/managers
- Salaries — Office staff
- Wages — Field workers
- Payroll taxes
- Owner retirement fund
- Employees' retirement fund
- Rent/lease/mortgage
- Heating fuel
- Water
- Electric
- Telephone
- Vehicle & equipment leases/payments
- Maintenance/repair — vehicles & equipment
- Gas/oil for vehicles
- Maintenance/repair — office equipment
- Interest expense
- Property tax
- Other taxes
- Licenses
- Insurance — liability
- Insurance — vehicles & other mechanical equipment
- Insurance — umbrella
- Insurance — performance bond (for trade contractors)
- Insurance — medical/dental
- Insurance — life
- Bad debts
- Collections expense
- Credit reports
- Legal expense
- Accounting expense

- Consultant expense
- Small tools
- Consumables (nails, screws, oil, grease, etc.)
- Advertising (broken down by media)
- Uniforms (if applicable)
- Selling/estimating expenses
- Business travel
- Office supplies'
- Postage
- Printing & copying
- Depreciation — building
- Depreciation — vehicles
- Depreciation — equipment
- Depreciation —tools
- Depreciation — office equipment
- Bank charges
- Returned checks
- Credit card charges
- Dues & subscriptions
- Donations
- Public Relations
- Freight
- Coffee/soft drinks/snacks for employees
- Discounted sales
- Education/seminars
- Customer gifts
- Miscellaneous

Don't let your "Miscellaneous" category get too bloated. If it starts creeping up beyond a couple of percentage points, break it down into more identifiable elements.

Paychecks Vs. Profits

Many business owners have a false conception of profit. They believe it equates with compensation, i.e., what the owner keeps after he pays his bills. By this reasoning, if a business doesn't turn any profit, the owner doesn't earn any money.

If the rest of the business world thought like that, hardly anyone would ever want to go into business. There's enough risk in putting at stake your underlying investment and good name. No need to make it so treacherous that you have to worry about where your next meal comes from.

That's why every owner should take a salary draw and build it into his/her pricing. This enables the owner to at least cover personal and family expenses while building the business. Relying on money that may or may not be there at the end is like going on combat patrol without a helmet and flak jacket.

Adding to the peril is the widespread practice of drawing a fairly small salary and paying oneself a large year-end bonus when times are good. Not only is this hard on family budgets, the IRS takes a dim view of oversized bonus distributions. The taxman may look at them as attempts to dodge corporate dividend payments, which are subject to both corporate and personal taxes. It's one of the top red flags used for singling out business owners for audits.

Take a cue from the big business world. CEOs and other executives of Fortune 500 companies take hefty salaries for themselves, commensurate with their job stature. Their oversized paychecks land in their bank accounts whether or not the business makes any money. When it does make money, they get compensated with bonuses that often are many times their salary. You never see big business executives and managers struggling to make ends meet until they turn a profit. Small business owners need to think the same way.

Profit has a purpose

Profit must be separated from income. The real purpose of profit is to provide capital for reinvestment, and/or to pay back loans you may have taken out to grow your business.

The business world likes to refer to profit as "retained earnings." The earnings get retained in order to fund business expansions, new buildings, new equipment, new services and other aspects of business growth. Whatever you can't fund out of retained earnings, you must borrow or pay out of your personal income. Funding it out of profits is the least painful way to go.

Profit also can be a source of profit sharing and bonus plans for both the owner and employees. In this sense profit can be part of owner compensation, but it should represent extra income as a reward for business success, not what you depend on to live day to day.

How much profit you build into your prices will be limited to a large extent by market restrictions on how much you can charge for your goods and services. The challenge is to allow for sufficient profit within reasonable market pricing by controlling your expenses. Keeping costs down is an essential component of running any business, but it should not come at the expense of profit, which is the lifeblood of any business.

Many owners of small closely-held businesses purposely hold down profits to avoid paying taxes on them. Small business owners would rather sink money into the business or spend it on owner and employee perks than pay almost a third of the profits to Uncle Sam.

I won't argue with this. It makes sense as long as it doesn't retard growth — and as long as you're confident you can justify all your perks to the IRS. Keep in mind, though, that avoiding taxes isn't the main purpose of being in business. Even if you have to pay Uncle Sam $3 out of every $10 you make in profit, that still leaves $7 to fund expansion and reinvest in the business and your people.

Paying taxes isn't the worst thing in the world. Avoiding taxes because you don't make any money is much worse.

Calculating profit

Whether your profit target is great or small, it's important to build profit into your selling prices. Here, I'm sorry to say, is where many small business owners make a fundamental mistake in arithmetic.

To illustrate, consider a sample problem, which was devised by my good friend Frank Blau, founder of Blau Sudden Service, one of Milwaukee's largest plumbing, heating and air conditioning firms that has succeeded in business since 1960. Frank retired from the business, now run by his sons, years ago and has spread business knowledge to thousands of small business owners, focusing on the nuts and bolts of business finance. He begins his seminars by asking attendees to come up with a selling price for a sample job. More than 90% typically come up with the wrong answer.

Suppose you offer a service for which you calculate the total cost to perform — including materials, labor and overhead — adds up to $1,000. You want to make a profit of 10%. How much do you have to sell that job for?

Most small business owners who attend Frank Blau's seminars mistakenly calculate the selling price as $1,100. They derive that amount by figuring profit as a percentage of cost, so that 10% of the total cost of $1,000 is $100, which they then add to the cost to come up with a selling price. However, profit must be calculated as a percentage not of cost, but of the final selling price. So, 10% profit on a job that costs out at $1,000 would require you to sell the job for $1,111.11. The math works out as follows:

Job cost = 90% of final selling price. 90% of X is equal to $1,000. To find X, the selling price, you need to <u>divide</u>, not multiply, $1,000 by 90%. $1,000/.90 = $1,111.11. Rather than going through the math for everything they sell, most business owners rely on a markup multiplication table like the one below.

Markup Table

5% added to cost is 4.75% profit
7.5% added to cost is 7% profit

10% added to cost is 9% profit
12.5% added to cost is 11.125% profit
15% added to cost is 13% profit
16.67% added to cost is 14.25% profit
17.5% added to cost is 15% profit
20% added to cost is 16.67% profit
25% added to cost is 20% profit
30% added to cost is 23% profit
33.33% added to cost is 25% profit
35% added to cost is 26% profit
37.5% added to cost is 27.25% profit
40% added to cost is 28.75% profit
45% added to cost is 31% profit
50% added to cost is 33.33% profit

Think of the implications of using incorrect markups. If a business owner bids our sample job at $1,100, thinking it includes 10% profit, in reality they are factoring in a net profit margin of only 9% and coming up short by more than $11 for every $1,000 in job cost.

This is one reason why many business owners are surprised when they can't seem to make ends meet even when the business appears to be doing pretty well.

That's A Good Idea, But I Can't Afford It!

Penny-pinching goes hand in hand with business start-ups. New business owners must keep expenses to a minimum. However, beware of false economies that can be as perilous to your business as overspending. Smart businesspeople make big mistakes when they aim to save money in the following areas:

Trade group memberships & education

Not every trade association is worthwhile, but belonging to an effective organization of similar businesses can enable a novice businessperson to greatly accelerate the learning curve in a particular field. Look for those that offer educational programs in areas where you might be deficient. Also, networking with non-competing colleagues in the same business can expose you to best practices to help you run your business better and make more money.

Some of these organizations charge hefty dues, but you tend to get the value you pay for. The question to ask is not how much it costs, but what are the potential benefits? Can they help you generate more money than the cost of membership? If so sign up as soon as possible.

Many business owners say they would like to join a trade group but want to wait until the business gets off the ground and they can afford it. *Stinkin' thinkin'!* The more successful you become, the less help you need. Join an organization at a time when they can help propel you to success.

Throughout my career I've attended over a thousand business seminars and workshops sponsored by trade associations or independent organizations. An interesting phenomenon I've noticed is that I always see some of the top people in the business attending these educational sessions. These wealthy and successful businesspeople know enough to teach the classes they attend, yet I would see them time after time listening intently to the instructors. Their reasoning is that if they come away with even one new idea, it could pay for the cost of their trip and then some.

These experienced pros are on to something. You may think you can't afford to take a day away from the business and pay several hundred bucks to sit in a seminar. Start thinking you can't afford not to.

Cheap stuff is expensive

Nothing is more expensive than cheap labor. Maybe from the start you can't afford to pay top dollar in wages, salaries and benefits, but the lowest-paying companies almost never end up as winners. Employee compensation is a foolish economy. Don't hire anyone until you're sure you can afford to, but when it's time pay enough to attract competent and reliable people. They will pay off in the long run – much more so than relying on bottom-rung employees and putting up with endless turnover.

Same goes for materials and equipment. Cutting corners with cheap materials is usually a recipe for callbacks and dissatisfied customers. Aging or second-hand equipment breaks down frequently, leading to performance failure, productivity decline and expensive repairs.

You get what you pay for. Lock that in as a mantra.

Pay bills on time

Besides customers and employees, suppliers are among your most important business relationships. They don't like waiting to get paid any more than you do, and the best way to damage a relationship with reputable suppliers is to leave them dangling. You jeopardize your credit rating doing that, and most businesses need to rely on credit at some point.

Many suppliers offer discounts up to a couple of percentage points for rapid payment, usually within 10 days of billing. This is free money! The only reason most business owners don't take advantage of these discounts is inadequate cash flow. Improve on the time it takes to collect your money and you'll realize an added bonus of being in position to take advantage of supplier discounts.

Marketing is essential

"Word of mouth is the best form of advertising." That old saying is true as far as it goes, but fails to account for a real world in which word of mouth usually doesn't spread far and fast enough to generate enough business to survive on. Advertising tends to be expensive yet it may also be essential for certain types of businesses to thrive.

Most people tend to use the terms marketing and advertising interchangeably. Advertising is just one component of marketing. Marketing encompasses advertising, communications and sales strategies. The most concise definition of marketing is that it's the process of identifying and satisfying customer needs and wants. My personal definition is that it's thinking up ways to persuade people to do business with you rather than competitors.

Think of how you can do that. How can you provide the best value in goods and services that your targeted customers look for? How can you communicate that to them?

Keep in mind that "USP" concept mentioned in Chapter 1. Most businesses have at least one Unique Selling Proposition though many business owners have trouble defining what their company does that is better or different than competitors. As food for thought, here are some potential USPs:

- **Longevity.** If your business has been around longer than most competitors, play it up. Longevity provides instant credibility. No business lasts a long time without leaving a lengthy trail of satisfied customers. "Since 1955" is a powerful statement that needs to be touted on all your signs, business cards, stationery and other marketing materials. The older the date, the more you should try to draw attention to it. (Always cite the date founded, not years in business, since that will increase as time passes and require constant updating of marketing materials.)

- **Awards & honors.** Many years ago Chicago Magazine had its food critic rank his favorite pizza restaurants in the city. Chicago is renowned for terrific pizza, but the critic's number one choice was a neighborhood joint that hardly anyone except people in that neighborhood knew about. After the article came out, people were standing in line every night to get into the little place that had only a handful of tables. Now, thanks in large measure to that magazine publicity, Giordano's grew to become a chain with numerous outlets throughout the city and suburbs. Few businesses are fortunate enough to be publicly recognized for excellence by a major metropolitan publication. But many of you have received smaller yet still notable honors within your local communities. Being named "Smithsville Chamber of Commerce Small Business of the Year" is something nobody else can claim. Make the most of these opportunities.

- **Convenient location.** This is about as simple as a USP gets and maybe more a matter of luck than calculation. But if it's relevant to your business ride it for all it's worth.
- **Testimonials.** Testimonials are perhaps the strongest marketing tool available to a business. That's because people patronize a business on the basis of trust more than anything else. They will believe friends, neighbors and fellow business owners who say good things about you.
- **Quantify performance.** Everyone says they sell the best goods or give top-notch service, so it goes in one ear and out the other with customers Quality is indeed a powerful USP, but proving it is the tricky part. What you need to do is figure out a way to quantify good performance.

One thought that comes to mind is the famous McDonald's slogan of "More than XX billion hamburgers sold," whatever the number might be these days. How about promoting your company as one with "Over x,xxx satisfied customers served."

Or, "More than xxxx jobs performed without a complaint."

Please don't just pick numbers out of thin air. It's easy enough to document the number of customers served or jobs performed simply by checking your records. How can you tell if they were satisfied? Well, just subtract the ones that complained about your services!

Whatever you do, don't lie. Lies always come back to haunt you. Besides, you don't need to fib. When you stop to think how many customers you've successfully served over the years, impressive numbers quickly add up.

- **Tout niche specialties.** A USP doesn't have to be literally "unique," meaning you are the only one in your market offering it. It could simply be a selective category of work that only a few other competitors offer. Are there certain materials or techniques you like to work with that most others don't? Is there something you do operationally that nobody else does? You can build a USP around these factors.

- **Build a special image.** McGuire Plumbing & Heating in the Twin Cities, MN, created a memorable image by dressing its service technicians in red neckties. Scottco Service Co. in Amarillo, TX, got a lot of mileage out of a jingle that went, "Uh oh, better call Scottco." Marketers of everything from cigarettes ("The Marlboro Man ... Joe Camel") to toilet paper ("Mr. Whipple") have capitalized on associating their products with fictional characters, slogans and tunes. It works. Once you have created a distinct identity, nobody can take it away from you. This makes it a USP.

Advertising gimmickry is of course no substitute for substance. To succeed in business, you still have to operate professionally and give good value. But sometimes you need a gimmick to create chances to show your stuff.

Chapter 3 – Every Business Is A People Business

Cultivate Quality Relationships

A struggling small-town lawyer attended his law school class reunion. The fellow eked out a modest living doing wills and real estate closings and was on a tight budget for the trip. He was humbled upon seeing a bunch of his former classmates in $3,000 suits driving expensive sports cars and ordering $100 bottles of wine with dinner. His classmates teased him about his lack of similar success.

A few years later the same small-town lawyer attended another class reunion, only this time he showed up with a driver and limo, wearing custom-made suits and weighed down by bling. "Wow, you've really come a long way since we last saw you," a law school friend remarked. "What changed?"

"Well," replied the small-town lawyer, "another attorney moved into town."

Normally I have as much regard for lawyers as I do for hair lice, and I never thought the day would come when I singled one out for praise. But that day arrived while speaking at a business conference years ago.

John Alfs was an attorney who preceded me on the program. He was a construction litigation specialist speaking to an audience of roofing contractors on the topic, "Protecting Yourself Through Intelligent Contracts." In doing so he made what may be the most profound sentence I've ever heard uttered in a business seminar:

"It's better to sign a bad contract with a good person than a good contract with a bad person."

No single sentence better summarizes the importance of sound business relationships. This un-lawyerly statement goes a long way towards defining a fundamental secret of success not only in construction but any other kind of business.

Swarming flies

A construction project nowadays comes attached with thousands of pages of legal mumbo-jumbo whose primary purpose is to shift responsibility from the party signing the contract to other parties, be they contractors, suppliers, project owners, architects, engineers, etc. But everyone involved plays the same game, and this creates endless opportunity for lawyers to craft disclaimers on behalf of their clients and dispute the validity of those protecting other parties. All for sizable fees, of course.

One of the insidious characteristics of the law business is that, unlike most businesses whose fortunes are restrained by demand for the goods they sell or the work they do, lawyers have the ability to create demand for their work. Any legal challenge compels a response from the parties challenged. Before you know it, you find lawyers swarming around a dispute like flies on you know what.

As a result, people in the construction business constantly complain about the amount of time they spend dealing with mind-numbing legal documents and trying to abide by their strictures. Most find themselves spending more time on legal nonsense than the productive things they are good at, such as running jobs and applying their craft. Alas, it's hard to get out from under the load of legalities when your own attorney keeps telling you the only way to protect yourself is to fire your own salvos of mumbo-jumbo.

How refreshing it was to hear that lawyer reveal his profession's dirty little secret. That is, no matter how airtight the contract language, it's no guarantee of prevailing in a legal dispute. Logic and precedent may or may not carry the day. Rulings are as likely to hinge on who hires the best attorney, or the best connected one, or which judge gets assigned the case, or what kind of mood that judge may be in on the day s/he hears your case.

Litigation seems to have replaced baseball as our national sport, and the attorneys all seem to be on steroids.

In construction, I've heard of certain general contractors whose business strategy is to bid jobs at cost or below, and count on high-octane legal staff to turn a profit after projects get underway. The money comes out of the hide of subcontractors and other members of the project team. How would you like to have your signature on a "good" contract with someone like that?

Poker vs. win-win

The complexities of construction invite more disputes than most other kinds of business. Buyers and sellers of merchandise may haggle over whether a broken item was sold that way or damaged after purchase, but it's pretty clear one or the other is at fault. In construction, if a building product or system doesn't work as it should, fingers point every which way among owners, general contractors, subcontractors, manufacturers, distributors, installers, designers, specifiers and more.

And then we rely on attorneys to straighten it all out, which is like recruiting arsonists to staff the fire department.

Contract language does not matter nearly as much as the character of the person holding the contract.

There are two basic philosophies of doing business. One is to view it like a poker game, with winners and losers. The other is to seek win-win scenarios where everyone manages to profit from their working relationships. Those are the relationships you want to cultivate.

Most construction contractors think of projects in terms of plans and specs and bidding procedures. Inexperienced or desperate contractors will take on virtually any job whose blueprints seem doable and that hold the promise of eking out a profit.

Wily veterans ask as many "who" as "what" questions about a proposed project. They refuse to work for certain GCs or owners under any circumstances.

When dealing with the right people, a handshake can be as binding as any legal document.

Are You A Good Boss?

The lawyer's tale just cited illustrates the importance of cultivating quality relationships with suppliers and customers. It's equally important to gain respect from the people you hire to work for you.

Being the boss is a pretty good feeling for most people. A certain satisfaction comes from calling the shots and being able to tell subordinates what to do. The boss usually gets paid more than the people s/he supervises and has more leeway in determining when and how to do the work that needs to be done. There may be extra perks as well, like a company car, club memberships, travel opportunities and so on.

Being the boss also carries special burdens. You get the blame when things go wrong. Sometimes you may have the unpleasant duty of telling people that they have to shape up. Worse, you may have to fire them when they don't. Worst of all, you may have to let some people go even though they didn't do anything wrong and may be good workers -- even friends -- simply because business conditions make it necessary to trim the payroll. Being the boss usually entails longer than normal working hours, and it's not always possible to stop thinking about work after you go home at night. Being the boss is stressful.

So, being the boss has its pluses and minuses. Good bosses tend to find a lot more pluses than minuses in their job. Bad bosses tend to be grumpy because they find the minuses outweigh the pluses.

What's it mean to be a good boss? To my way of thinking, the simplest definition means finding the appropriate balance between the needs of the business and the needs of the employees you supervise. These are not mutually exclusive.

The needs of the business must be first and foremost in the mind of any boss. If your business doesn't succeed, the people who work for you will be out of their jobs. No matter how well you treat them, no matter how much they may like you, you're not doing them any favors by putting their needs above those of the business if it leads to the business no longer being able to support them.

However, some bosses go so far overboard looking out for the bottom line of their businesses that they ride roughshod over their workers. This makes them bad bosses. Bosses that treat their people badly are hurting more than helping the business. This may not be apparent when business is booming and the company is making money even though employee morale may be low. But it comes back to bite the company when a downturn comes.

Bad bosses increase employee turnover, and turnover exacts a severe cost. Each new person costs thousands of dollars to hire and train, and it may take months or even years for a new employee to become fully productive.

Moreover, turnover can turn cancerous. Disgruntled employees who quit or get fired depart with bad feelings, and they will vent those feelings to everyone they know. Employees that remain will worry about their jobs and may sympathize with the staffers who left. Word spreads that your business is a lousy place to work, which will diminish your ability to hire good people to work for you.

So, what's it take to be a good boss? In my estimation, the best bosses are leaders rather than managers. The difference has to do with a famous observation that I believe originated with Peter Drucker – *Managers gain power from above, leaders from below.*

The fact that you own your business or have been appointed to a managerial position gives you the authority to tell people what to do. But it doesn't guarantee maximum effort or results on their part. People will perform tasks assigned by a manager because they have to. They'll do it for a leader because they want to, and they'll do the best job they can. The leader has a knack for convincing them that it's in their best interest to perform to the max. Sometimes they'll even go all out just to please a leader because they revere him or her, just like a child wanting to make Mom and Dad proud.

All of which begs the question, what makes for a good leader? Many books have been written about this subject, and I can't hope to explain it all in a few paragraphs. But here are some elements of leadership that I believe are paramount.

- **Never ask a subordinate to do something you can't or won't do yourself.**

Leaders project confidence that stems from knowing what they are talking about and how to do the job they ask others to do. Businesses that promote from within usually have this facet covered because the supervisors have hands-on, "been there, done that" experience. It's a bigger problem with large companies that recruit people with MBAs and other professional management credentials, but who may have little inkling of the nuts and bolts work done by the company.

- **Be open to advice from below.**

The legendary U.S. Army General George S. Patton once stated, "Never tell people how to do things. Tell them what to do and they will surprise you with their ingenuity."

Micromanaging is a prime characteristic of bad bosses. People who are on the front lines usually have the best feel for how to accomplish their work most effectively. Listen carefully to your salespeople, your work crews in the field, your office staff processing the paperwork. Don't just listen passively, ask them for their input regularly. Put a system in place to share extra pay with them for ideas that save money. Sometimes their ideas are unworkable or cost too much. But just listening to them has morale-boosting merit, and when their ideas pan out, the business comes out ahead. I bet you'll find a high percentage of recommendations generated by workers do prove to be good ones.

When speaking with subordinates, be aware of how much talking you do and how much comes from them. If you are doing most of the talking, shut up and listen.

- **Give credit freely.**

One of the fastest ways for a boss to become disliked is to take excessive credit for ideas or work contributed by subordinates. Top-notch quarterbacks always pay tribute to their receivers and offensive line. Be sure to single out every employee who had a hand in a job well done.

- **Share the wealth – and the pain.**

A pat on the back works even better when accompanied by extra pay. When employees come up with ideas to save money, make sure they are rewarded commensurately.

Or, get creative with rewards. Wool Supply is a distributor of plumbing supplies based in Ft. Lauderdale, Florida, that blew me away with a rewards program unlike any I've heard of in my years covering the small business world.

Ever since the early years of the business, the company got into the habit of shutting down operations for up to a week each year to indulge employees and spouses with a company trip, all expenses paid. Not just for managers or sales contest winners, but truck drivers, warehouse workers, office staff — everyone got invited to these excursions. The trips started out as overnights, then expanded into three-day cruises (Ft. Lauderdale being the nation's cruise capital), and in some years they've gone away for an entire week. To celebrate the company's 50th anniversary in 2007, Wool Supply treated all employees and spouses to a week-long visit to London, England. Some 150 people participated.

Keep in mind that not only did the company pay for the excursions, their business shut down for up to a week. They notified their customers in advance and encourage them to stock up, but owner Randy Wool acknowledged they may end up losing some business while everyone is away. "I feel the benefits outweigh the risks," he told me. "I'm not aware of any other company that does this for all employees, and having happy employees is the key to success in our business."

By the same principle, bosses need to cut back their lifestyles amid cutbacks and layoffs when times are tough. During the bleak recession of the late 2000s, the public at-large got infuriated at large bonuses paid to bankers and the Wall Street crowd while ordinary people were losing their jobs or taking steep cuts in pay. Small business employees feel the same way when they see their bosses showing off new cars and taking lavish vacations while they are told to tighten their belts in order to hold onto their jobs.

- **Take the heat.**

A good leader never passes the buck. One of the best examples of this comes from the historical record:

"Our landings in the Cherbourg-Havre area have failed to gain a satisfactory foothold and I have withdrawn the troops. My decision to attack at this time and place was based on the best information available. The troops, the air (corps) and the Navy did all that bravery and devotion to duty could do. If any blame or fault attaches to that attempt, it is mine alone."

This message was composed by Gen. Dwight D. Eisenhower on June 6, 1944. It's what he would have told the press and public had the D-Day invasion failed. Happily, he instead broadcast a different message announcing a successful landing on the beaches of Normandy. This contingency note, however, reveals much about the character of this great leader who subsequently became our 34th President of the United States. If the D-Day invasion had not succeeded, there would have been plenty of blame to go around since various people would have fed Ike wrong information or fallen short in military performance. Instead, he chose to take it all upon his shoulders, and this never-delivered message stands as a beacon of leadership.

- **Praise in public, criticize in private.**

When someone does something well, say it out loud or put it in writing for the entire company to see. When it comes time to correct an employee, do it one-on-one and keep it between the two of you. If it's a serious mistake that others need to be know about in order to avoid a repeat, focus on the incident, not the person who made the mistake, who should remain anonymous in anything written about the event.

"A mistake was made that cost us a bunch of money."
NOT: *"Joe made a mistake that cost us a bunch of money."*

- **Keep doors open.**

A complete open-door policy is impractical in a very large organization. The CEO of a Fortune 500 company can't very well invite tens of thousands of employees to barge into his office whenever they feel like it. But if that CEO is a good leader, he'll have systems in place to assure that the concerns and ideas of even the lowliest employees have a way of filtering all the way to the top.

Most of you reading this work for businesses small enough that it is possible for the top executive to speak directly with every employee from time to time. I accompanied the aforementioned Randy Wool on visits to three company branches and witnessed him greeting every desk clerk, truck driver and forklift operator by their first name, as they did him. He asked several about family members by name and chatted with each one like an old friend. It's no coincidence that the business, started by his father Carl Wool, has lasted more than half a century and shows no signs of fading.

"Our strength as an independent distributor is that our employees feel like they are part of the organization and their voices get heard," Randy commented. "The larger the organization, the more distant people are from management and the owners."

"People want to be seen and appreciated," Ellen Rohr observed. "That's more important than money to many of them. They value the ability to succeed in their job."

- **Don't get TOO close.**

Leaders need to be likable and accessible to the people they supervise, but it's awkward to become best buddies with them. This is why the U.S. military discourages off-duty fraternizing between officers and enlisted personnel. Mission performance can be compromised when someone is called upon to put a close friend in harm's way.

You may not be dealing with life and death matters in your

business, but from time to time hard decisions may have to be made that put people in harm's way with regard to employment or compensation. Those decisions become excruciating when it's a buddy to whom you have to deliver bad news.

Plus, appearances of favoritism can reduce a boss's effectiveness with the rest of the staff. The situation becomes even stickier when close friendships arise between bosses and subordinates of the opposite sex. Even if the relationship is platonic, tongues are bound to start wagging.

- **Cut some slack with personal issues.**

A good boss will do whatever s/he can to help out employees deal with personal or family problems. We live in a world filled with working moms, people taking care of elderly parents or faced with various other difficulties outside of work. This doesn't excuse people from doing the job they are paid to do. Yet if there is any way to accommodate them with time off, flexible hours, or other considerations that don't harm business operations very much, it will pay off in the long run.

There's a delicate balance involved here, however. Some people will view special favors as an open door to take advantage of you and concoct other excuses for special treatment. This kind of behavior needs to be cut off when you feel you're being played for a sucker.

Also keep in mind that you can't show favoritism. If you make special allowances for one employee, you need to do it for everyone in similar circumstances. And you have to do it in a way that doesn't impact business performance. All that being said, good leaders understand that cutting some slack on occasion usually results in those people paying back with extra effort.

Is Your Business A Great Place To Work?

Davis & Warshow, based in Maspeth, a Long Island suburb of New York City, is another long-lasting plumbing distributor hailed as among the best in its industry. When I went to interview President Frank Finkel for a story I wrote about the family-owned company in 2003, I expected to be escorted into a plush executive suite like so many others I had luxuriated in throughout my career. Instead I got taken to what more closely resembled a mosh pit.

Finkel's "executive suite" consisted of a small desk and computer terminal no different than those of dozens of other managers and office staffers in a communal front office. Their work spaces were arranged just a few feet apart without even cubicle dividers. Rank and status were invisible, job functions fluid, privacy impossible and vocal chords the main instrument of corporate communication, which was thick with banter. Not only did the company honchos work in beehive fashion, most days they lunched together in a conference room on company-paid grub from a local deli.

"This routine has been our persona since the days of Mr. Davis and Mr. Warshow," Finkel told me, referring to the company's founders and namesakes. (Frank's father, Irving Finkel, acquired the company from Davis & Warshow long ago.) "I think it's a lot of fun. Most of us are in here for more than eight hours a day, and some of us put in more than twelve hours. Working together like this in close quarters enables us to help out one another a lot better than if we had private offices and cubicles with no interaction. And we put some humor into it, which makes for an enjoyable day.

"It also makes for a more productive day, because the ebb and flow of conversation enables all of us to learn something new every day. Guys will talk about visiting a customer, and you learn things about that customer and maybe some competitors. Things that go on in this 'fur ball' of an office help us become better at what we do," Frank Finkel said.

A "one for all, all for one" egalitarian spirit pervades the company's ranks. I interviewed more than a half-dozen D & W personnel for my story, and without prompting, just about all of them expressed joy working for this company.

Observed vice president of sales Alan Cohen: "People here are compensated well, not in random fashion, but based on how well they produce. That's a great tool for shaping performance. Plus, we're surrounded by a lot of nice people, and that makes it enjoyable when you spend 11 to 12 hours at work."

I've visited hundreds of different businesses ranging from huge manufacturing plants to tiny mom and pop shops. Usually I can sense within a few minutes of the visit whether this is an organization that's good to work for. Nuances in employee behavior reveal whether they feel comfortable and enjoy their job.

Good organizations come in all shapes, sizes and cultures. Some operate with a very formal business-like atmosphere, and some so loosely it seems the inmates are running the asylum. Some have strict dress codes and a lot of other rules governing employee behavior, while others remind me of a rowdy bar on Saturday night. Some bosses/owners have a hands-on management style, others are somewhat aloof.

These define corporate cultures, but a corporate culture is to some extent a superficial characteristic of a business. Different personalities may fit better in one type of organization than another, but the traits I'm about to discuss transcend corporate culture. Whatever the culture, here are certain characteristics that make a company or organization a great place to work, as follows.

- **People are busy.**

This may seem counterintuitive, but I've noticed a correlation between employee morale and the amount of work they have to do — and it's the opposite of what many people might think. People who are busy at work, even "overworked," tend to be happier than those with too much time to kill.

There's a limit to the workload you can expect out your people, of course, but it's better for them to be busy at productive tasks than figuring out ways to look busy so they can keep their jobs. When employees have to stretch themselves to do their jobs, they feel needed, secure and motivated. Idle time gets accompanied by whining, gossip, rumors and intrigue.

When people are busy, the organization is likely to be doing well financially. This leads to raises, promotions and job security, all of which make people happy. At some point your people may be so busy it's time to hire more of them. But first make sure your heavy workload is sustainable over the long term. Nothing is more devastating to morale than layoffs and panicky cost-cutting.

At some point you can cross the line between challenging your associates and burning them out. A good staffing philosophy is to make sure your employees have to put in longer than normal hours when work is at a peak. They can do this for days or weeks at a time. When overtime (paid or unpaid) becomes more the rule than the exception, it's time to hire more help.

- **Employees are empowered.**

Don't you hate to deal with a business where everyone you talk to has to consult a superior or pass you along to someone else before you get your problem solved? Anyone who deals with customers ought to have a reasonable degree of authority to make decisions that help customers, even if those decisions cost money. Even low-ranking clerical people ought to be able to make $100 decisions using their own best judgment.

- **Marketing makes people happy.**

One would seem to have nothing to do with the other, but people seem happier in companies that do a lot of advertising and marketing than in organizations that don't. It's because people feel proud to be associated with organizations that are visible and well known. They also will be quick to recruit talented friends and associates to work for a firm they believe is a good place to work.

- **No chicken bleep rules.**

Every business needs to have rules, and rules need to be enforced in order to avoid workplace chaos. This doesn't mean you need a rule for every little thing, and it doesn't mean every rule needs to be enforced to the letter. For instance, if an employee habitually comes in early and stays late, does it really make sense to call that person on the carpet for taking 15 minutes longer than allowed for lunch break?

Years ago I visited a company shortly after management came out with a policy forbidding employees from decorating their work spaces with photos and other personal effects. Everyone was in a foul mood over the pointless rule. It came about from one of the siblings who owned the business and was assigned the role of office manager, probably because he was too stupid to be trusted with financial or customer duties. He took that to mean that his job was to think up chicken bleep rules that made life miserable for the people who had made his family's business successful.

Nordstrom's department store is famous for its customer service and regarded as one of the best places to work in the retail industry. Its employee handbook has a section headed "Rules," which reads as follows:

"Use your best judgment at all times. There are no other rules."

You need to trust the judgment of the people on your payroll. If you don't feel you can trust them, why in the world did you hire them, and why are you keeping them on the payroll?

- **Flex time rocks!**

Time off means more to many people than extra money in today's hectic world. Often they need time off from work to deal with child or elder care issues.

Businesses cannot allow everyone to take off whenever they want, but flexible work schedules are a great trade-off wherever practical. Many jobs involving paperwork can be performed at any time of day without hurting the business. Some working moms might find it more convenient to work split shifts that allow them to depart for several hours in order to drop kids off and pick them up at school. Companies that allow flex time schedules usually have happy and motivated work forces.

Flexible hours may not be practical for every job, but think again about the concept of employee empowerment. When in doubt ask your people if they could get the job done working flexible hours. Then trust their judgment.

- **Have fun.**

You don't need to throw parties — although once in a while that might not be a bad idea. What you do need to do, though, is create an atmosphere where a little good-natured humor and banter becomes part of the daily routine.

A relaxed working atmosphere adds rather than detracts from productivity. People who like one another and kid around are likely to share information and lend a helping hand. As the boss, make it a point to smile as much as possible throughout the day, and be generous with compliments.

There need to be boundary lines, of course. Having fun at work cannot be allowed to degenerate into physical horseplay or intrude upon customer contacts. Banter cannot deteriorate into insults or sexual innuendo. Even if every person except one regards something as inoffensive, that one killjoy has the power of making life miserable for everyone in the company.

Nonetheless, it's still possible to have fun without offending anyone. A good rule of thumb about humor is always to poke fun at oneself, never at anyone else.

A good place to work is all about feeling good about the people you work with and the surrounding environment. Think about this — many people spend more waking hours at their workplace than they do with their loved ones. How they react to that environment has a lot to do with how productive they may be.

Constructive Criticism

Most small business owners and managers pulled themselves up by the proverbial bootstraps. They got where they are through hard work and endurance. They are not known for touchy-feely sensitivity. Blue collar trades in particular have a tradition of gruff, straight-shooting relations between supervisors and subordinates. This culture can be summed up by some of the short phrases commonly used in orienting new employees:

- *"It's my way or the highway."*
- *"I may not always be right, but I'm always the boss."*
- *"Keep messing up and I'll bleepety bleep your sorry bleep to kingdom come!"*

Maybe you're a little more sensitive than these stereotypes suggest. But there are way too many owners and managers for whom conflict with employees is the rule rather than the exception. I've heard certain bosses complain that the worst part of their job is dealing with subordinates. That's a signal that they were lacking in the interpersonal skills needed to be an effective business manager. I bet the people who work for them would say the worst part of their jobs is dealing with the boss.

Frequently, conflict in the workplace arises out of criticism, either between supervisors and subordinates or co-workers of equal stature. But criticism sometimes is necessary. What's important is to understand the difference between constructive criticism and the destructive kind that results from simply lashing out because of anger or frustration.

Here are some guidelines to assure that criticism becomes constructive rather than destructive in the workplace.

- **Understand the difference between criticism and discipline.**

Criticism is aimed at correcting honest mistakes or minor infractions. Discipline is a more serious step taken to change performance or behavior that can lead to termination if repeated. Every human is subject to criticism on occasion, but not everyone needs to be disciplined.

- **Criticize the action, not the person.**

The fact that someone made a mistake doesn't make that person bad or incompetent. The best among us will make mistakes from time to time.

A good thing to do in this regard is to couple criticism with statements that boost self-esteem.

"Ordering the wrong material cost us quite a bit of time and money. These catalogs are so confusing, it's easy to see how someone could goof up. Be extra careful next time you order."

- **Be specific, and don't exaggerate.**

"This is the third time you've been late this month" can be presented as an indisputable fact. "You're *always* coming in late" is the kind of statement likely to get the guilty party thinking, "What's this idiot talking about, I've only been late three times this month!"

Similarly, be sure that job performance can be measured in concrete terms. Insisting on "quality workmanship" will only lead to interpretations and arguments. You have to use specific measures such as defects reported, time spent on rework, etc.

- **Be sure the behavior you're criticizing can be changed.**

The owner of a plumbing company once told me of a newly hired dispatcher who seemed to be doing a terrific job, except she had an aversion to paperwork. She always made excuses not to do it, and when pressed made a mess of it.

Turns out she had dyslexia. This never came out in the job interview. Because she otherwise did commendable work, the owner kept her employed and organized her job in a way that paperwork was minimized and could be performed by someone else.

- **Use the word "we" rather than "you."**

"We need to turn in job tickets promptly" is a better way of saying it than, "You need to turn in job tickets promptly." Doesn't sound so accusatory.

In another context, "we" is better than "I" when it comes to criticizing a co-worker or subordinate. "We think you need to do better" is a more powerful statement than "I think you need to do better." If the criticism comes from two sources, such as the owner and a supervisor, it's harder for an employee to dismiss it than if only one party expresses displeasure. Single-source criticism can be rationalized as someone "picking on me … a personality conflict … s/he's just in a bad mood."

- **Give reasons for the criticism.**

"We need to turn in job tickets promptly, because otherwise paychecks will get delayed." Young people in particular do not like to blindly follow orders. They want to know *why* they are expected to do things a certain way.

- **Anger, sarcasm, raised voices are never appropriate.**

Sports fans like me get amused by the temper tantrums thrown by baseball managers, football and basketball coaches in response to disputed umpire/referee calls. Many of them do it for show in order to influence subsequent calls in their teams' favor.

Apart from a field of play, this kind of behavior is unprofessional and likely to have more negative than positive consequences. This includes severely negative potential outcomes like violence or lawsuits by beleaguered employees. Recognize overbearing behavior for what it is and regard the control of emotions as a sign of professionalism.

Bosses also have a special obligation to avoid gossip and complaining. Whiners and rumor mongers are corrosive to any organization. The people in charge need to set good examples with their own behavior, and put a stop to it when done by subordinates.

- **Don't belabor the point.**

Constructive criticism is short and sweet, not a lecture. Make your point, document the problem with a short note in the employee's file, then move on.

- **Cool off before putting it in writing.**

Sometimes criticism needs to be conveyed in writing. But do so only after a decent interval that allows you to collect your thoughts and anger to dissipate. Writing something down provides a permanent record, for better or worse, of your state of mind. It could come back to haunt you.

Written criticism (again, differentiated from discipline) should be coupled with expressions of confidence and support of the recipient, i.e.—

"In general, you've done a fine job and I'm sure you'll continue to be a valuable employee, but you need to take care to avoid incidents like …"

- **NEVER, EVER criticize in public.**

Sorry to be repetitive, but it's worth repeating. Praise in public, criticize in private. Make this a management mantra to live by and instill in all of your supervisors.

Seniority Isn't Always What It's Cracked Up To Be

Turn to the help wanted ads and you'll see listing after listing asking for "three years experience … minimum five years experience."

It's right to value experience. Common sense tells us that people with experience generally require less training and know more tricks of their trade than people who haven't been around as long. Yet the biggest value of experience comes in the form of wisdom more than knowledge.

Knowledge means having a grasp of myriad details applicable to any given job. A lot of novice whiz kids can surpass veterans when it comes to technical know-how. That's especially true in our information age where youngsters who have grown up with computers generally have a lot more technological savvy than old-timers.

What we old-timers generally have over the youngsters is a knack for identifying which details are most important in any given situation, and when certain methods may or may not work. This is where wisdom comes in. Knowledge is recognizing a good poker hand. Wisdom is sensing when to hold and when to fold. Wisdom more often than not correlates with experience.

Respect for elders is one of our culture's most enduring values. We owe a debt of gratitude to those who came before us. I will not belittle the value of experience. It's the reason I'm writing this book.

All this being said, be careful about going overboard in deference to veteran employees. I feel like a traitor to my demographic group in saying so, but longevity doesn't automatically confer knowledge, wisdom or competence. Sometimes longtime employees are as much a hindrance as an asset.

People with a lot of seniority often adhere to outmoded ideas and are reluctant to accept much-needed change. They are apt to do things a certain way simply because "that's the way we've always done it." Some have trouble adapting to computer technology and the internet, which have important roles in almost every business nowadays.

This is not to suggest you should look to get rid of all the old folks and replace them with energetic youngsters. For one thing, that could leave you vulnerable to an age-discrimination lawsuit. Plus, you don't want to throw out the baby with the bath water; most veterans do possess a storehouse of knowledge and institutional memory you wouldn't want to dispense with. The problem is that in too many small organizations, seniority has become the ONLY criterion for advancement. You make good old Joe the manager or foreman because he's been there the longest. Maybe it's also because he's slowing down a bit with the physical load. Sometimes you know deep down that he's not the best person for the job, but you feel obliged to reciprocate loyalty for his many years of service. Besides, you think Joe couldn't handle being supervised by someone half his age.

You should indeed reciprocate loyalty, reward seniority and accommodate veteran employees who may be breaking down physically. But you want to do it in ways that don't alienate the young talent in your organization or hamper your company's ability to progress. This requires playing to everyone's individual strengths, young and old alike.

For instance, some folks are "people persons" and some are not. Many mechanically minded individuals are happiest when they are solving technical problems rather than supervising smart aleck youngsters or dealing with paperwork. You don't want to put someone like that in charge of managing other people. Yet, that's what is routinely done throughout our economy. In small and big businesses alike, many people get promoted simply because "it's their turn."

In many cases, it's all about money. After all, you can't expect to pay your best salesman more than his manager makes, can you?

Why not?

To which I would answer, why not? It may be that the salesman is more valuable and irreplaceable than the person he reports to. If that's the case, it makes more sense to pay him more than to suffer the alternative of weakening yourself in two positions – by taking the salesman away from that which he does best, and promoting him to a supervisory job that he may hate and is ill equipped to handle.

Keep in mind that professional football coaches and baseball managers typically get paid a lot less than their star players. The good ones still manage to teach and motivate. Supervisory positions have a lot of advantages — desk job, more prestige, steadier hours, less physically demanding — that many people would view as an acceptable trade-off with income.

When you do promote younger employees to supervisory positions, it's important to instruct them to be especially deferential to company veterans. Encourage them to ask their advice frequently. In some cases, it may be necessary to come up with a reporting structure in which the veteran reports directly to the owner.

More often than not, experienced employees will probably get the nod for promotions by virtue of merit, because experience does have value. The point is, age and experience should not be the sole deciding factor in who gets promoted.

Is It Ethical To "Steal" Employees?

At the time of this writing the business media was reporting on some big corporations that have come under fire for policies that prohibit hiring people who are unemployed. It stems from a "survival of the fittest" belief that people let go are likely to be among the least capable employees. So, certain companies instruct their human resources staffs to recruit people exclusively from those already working, especially hiring them from competitors.

I can't support such policies. A lot of top-notch people get laid off for reasons that have nothing to do with performance or behavior issues. Some fall victim to mergers/acquisitions or seniority policies, others worked for business units that were shut down or severely cut back, or they may have quit voluntarily for personal reasons. A blanket policy of not hiring anyone unemployed is stupidly rigid.

Yet, there is a kernel of truth to the belief that you are more likely to find capable people already with jobs than without. Common sense tells you that the best people don't stay unemployed for long, and that a history of frequent job changes is a sensible red flag when making hiring decisions.

I've observed in many small businesses an opposite tenet. Many small business owners consider it unethical to "steal" a competitor's employee. They present it as a moral issue, but I don't buy that. This is America, and America is about freedom for both employers and employees. The term "stealing" an employee suggests ownership, but ever since President Lincoln's Emancipation Proclamation in 1863, nobody in this country has held ownership rights over any other human being. We are all free agents, and if you have the wherewithal to treat people better than another employer, you have every right to make them an offer.

In most cases, businesses invoke ethics and morality to disguise the real reason they resist hiring people away from competitors. It's the fear that a competitor may do the same to them. Nobody wants to get into an employee bidding war, so competitors establish unwritten agreements not to go after one another's people.

This philosophy may have other tangled motives. Local competitors sometimes belong to the same trade association and may be social friends. Then it boils down to a business decision weighing company needs versus the value of the friendship. You may decide that a personal relationship is more important than your business interest, and that's okay. Just understand that this does not make it a moral issue.

An odd thing about the "don't steal employees" rule never is that it never seems to apply except between direct competitors. If a local business hires someone away from a similar business in a different market, nobody looks at it as doing anything wrong. It's just when you hire someone from a company that competes against you that it somehow seems against the unwritten rule. Can anyone find any logic in this?

In any case, the way to ensure that nobody does it to you is simply to treat your employees better than your competitors. Hiring good people is only half of the success equation. The other half is keeping them.

Golden rules of retaining good people

If you focus on keeping the good people you have, you'll automatically create the kind of company that will also attract the best people working for someone else in your local marketplace. At the same time, you'll insulate yourself against competitors hiring your best people away, simply because you offer better jobs than they do. And, you'll reduce cancerous turnover.

Better jobs don't automatically correlate with highest pay, although pay scales certainly need to be competitive. Business owners frequently gripe about disloyal employees who jump ship because a competitor offered them a few bucks more. My first thought is they must be lousy managers if their people are so willing to leave for a few extra bucks.

Here are some ways to make your working environment an attractive one for employees who may be getting wooed by competitors.

- **Be generous with praise and recognition.**

Various surveys show that employees rank recognition and "being appreciated" even higher than pay in their evaluation of desirable employment.

TD Industries is a large mechanical contracting firm based in Dallas that year after year lands on Fortune magazine's list of the nation's best employers. I wrote an article about TD years ago and witnessed a lot of things they do to earn these honors. One that remains etched in my mind is their "Wall of Honor."

It's in a handsome wood-paneled alcove near the main reception area of their headquarters facility. Subdued lighting and the absence of intrusive decor gives it the ambience of a chapel. The focal point of the room was the designated "Wall of Honor" featuring dozens of professionally photographed pictures of every past and present TD employee who has worked for the company at least five years. They were arranged not by management hierarchy, but tenure. Employees who had worked there the longest were in the top rows no matter where they fit in the corporate ranks.

When I visited the most honored positions belonged to the founder and, next to him, a foreman who had been with the company for something like 35 years. The foreman's photograph occupied a more prominent position than those of the corporate executives then leading the company, because they hadn't been there as long.

TD's pay scales were not extraordinary by industry standards. Numerous surveys have shown that money does not rank at the top of what employees crave in their jobs. Ranking higher are respect and the feeling that they are making a valuable contribution.

- **Be generous with compensation.**

I just said that money doesn't count for everything, but that doesn't mean it doesn't count for anything. You don't need to be the highest paying company in your area to instill loyalty, but you need to be closer to the top than the bottom.

Note the term "compensation." This encompasses pay and benefits. You can pay a little less in wages and salaries and still attract great employees if you offer a first-class health care package, retirement program and other benefits, such as flexible work schedules.

Common sense tells you that you get what you pay for, in anything. Usually there's a direct correlation between the amount of money made by a company and the caliber of its people. Compensate them accordingly.

- **Practice open-book management.**

Privately-owned businesses prefer to keep the financial details of their business secret except to owners (usually family members). The prevailing attitude is that it's nobody's business how much money you make.

Literally true, I suppose. However, the best companies are those whose employees behave as if they own it. You don't necessarily have to cut employees in on a piece of the action. It's just that an open-book management system has the effect of making employees feel a sense of ownership and a stake in the company's success.

Simply show your people the company's P & L statement. This documents for them how important it is to keep expenses under control and profits up. Even better, create some sort of incentive compensation plan so that all employees share in the company's prosperity.

You don't need to show them every last detail of the company's finances. For instance, they don't need to know how much the owner makes in income. Such details can be buried in general administrative expense categories. But it helps to make them feel part of your team if you show them how the company is doing on a regular basis.

After our economy hit the skids in the late 2000s, most companies enacted painful layoffs and expense cutbacks. Open-book companies on the whole managed to endure better than most because their employees understood the financial difficulties. Many of these businesses were able to keep everyone employed thanks to employees agreeing to pay cuts and/or reduced hours. Sharing financial information also helps to spur cost-cutting ideas throughout the ranks. This happens when people pull together as a team, and open books help foster a team spirit.

- **Be slow to hire, and slow to fire.**

The boom and bust cycle is one of the biggest drawbacks to the construction industry. Lack of job security leads many trade workers to go into business for themselves in order to avoid layoffs. I've met numerous contractors over the years who make less money than the people working for them. They're just happy they never have to worry about being laid off.

A business can't carry excessive employees forever, which is why you are well advised to go slow in hiring new people. Make sure everyone is working at peak capacity before you take anyone on, just in case a slowdown catches you by surprise. Explain to your people that though you're working them hard, the more people on the payroll, the less there is to go around for everyone else. Before you hire someone else, make sure your business will support them for more than the month or two.

- **Spread choice perks.**

Share with employees tickets to sports and entertainment events, convention trips, restaurant dinners, etc. It's especially effective when the spouse gets to share in the reward.

Be fair with these, however. They have to be perceived by all employees as a reward for exceptional performance, or else given to everyone on a rotational basis. It would be counterproductive to have perks perceived by employees as favoritism.

- **One bad apple can spoil the bunch.**

Nobody wants to be too quick to fire anyone, but a bad employee can poison your well for everyone. Employees resent it when the boss covers up for a non-performer or someone who habitually breaks rules that apply to all. Firing a problem employee who's been around for a long time can be traumatic, but you'd be surprised at how many others will feel better and work harder after you do the dirty deed.

With a lot of small businesses, the problem employee may be a relative. Speaking as a loving father and grandfather, I support the right of small business owners to put relatives on their payroll even if they are not world-class workers. Just understand that nothing is as destructive to employee morale as a family member who's overpaid and not pulling his/her weight.

One small business owner I know confided in me that he told all of his children they were entitled to a job in the company he owned, but not to a title. That they would have to earn. One of his sons was serving as company president, and another headed up operations. A third son, who happened to be the oldest among them, apparently had some personal issues and was employed as a truck driver. This may have made for some awkward family dynamics, but I admired the owner for sticking to his principle.

- **Be on guard against the Peter Principle.**

"The Peter Principle" is a term coined by the 1969 best-selling book of the same title by Larry Peters and Raymond Hull. It describes the tendency of people in an organizational hierarchy to get promoted until they surpass their ability to do the job. It explains why top-notch workers often become poor managers.

The Peter Principle is a phenomenon that has been confirmed both by academic research and real-world observations by almost everyone who has worked for a length of time in a large organization. A corollary from the original book is not as widely cited but filled with meaning: "work is accomplished by those employees who have not yet reached their level of incompetence." In other words, incompetent supervisors can be made to look good by capable subordinates. This speaks volumes about why workers frequently resent their bosses.

What it says to you as a small business owner or manager is, don't use promotions as an automatic reward for good performance.

First make sure the person is capable of handling the elevated position, and even wants it. Sometimes they don't. If they do, then do what you can to make sure they can handle the additional responsibilities.

The insidious thing about The Peter Principle is that it weakens your business in two ways – by taking a competent performer away from a job s/he does well, and promoting the person to a job that may be even more important but which s/he is incapable of performing.

The Golden Rule

Managing employees is not something that comes naturally to most business owners. A hard-driven, risk-taking entrepreneur can't relate very well to security-conscious employees obsessed with steady paychecks and working conditions. Yet inevitably comes a point when the entrepreneur builds a business large enough that s/he has to rely on other employees in order to function.

Some businesses rely on expensive machinery, and no owner would ever think of hiring someone to operate complex machines without extensive experience or training in their operation. Yet it's common for small businesses to put humans in charge of the most complicated machinery of all – other people – with little if any training and direction. Throughout the business world we repeatedly see the top sales rep get promoted to sales manager, the best mechanic named foreman, a super numbers cruncher put in charge of the accounting department and so on. While they have proven themselves capable of doing the work itself, this does not automatically qualify them to lead other people in those tasks. Many of them get promoted to supervisory positions without a single minute of supervisory training.

So, what can you do about it? Sending supervisors to people management classes and seminars is not at all a bad thing to do. Yet even in the absence of formal training, there is a simple people management program available to everyone that can be easily implemented at a moment's notice. What's more, it's free.

A moral imperative

It's called The Golden Rule (TGR), and we've all heard of it: *Do unto others as you would have them do unto you.* In a pinch TGR can substitute for formal management training. In fact, be wary of any management system that doesn't have it as a core value.

TGR comes from the New Testament, but one doesn't have to be a Christian to recognize its wisdom and moral roots. No matter what the job might be, you get better performance out of people by treating them well than by kicking tail. If you want academic studies to verify that, spend a little time searching the internet and you'll find plenty of research showing that you get better results with positive than negative motivational techniques.
Just think of it as common sense. And, think of it as the right thing to do.

It's unfashionable nowadays to speak of morality. It makes many people uncomfortable. The beautiful thing about TGR is it serves double-duty as a moral imperative and profit-generating business principle.

TGR says that when any question arises about how to deal with a person, ask yourself how you would want to be treated in the same circumstance. TGR says you have a responsibility to give fair value to customers in return for the money they pay you, and that you must pay bills on time for those who do the same to you. Do that, and people will enjoy buying from and selling to you.

TGR also holds you responsible for providing fair pay and benefits to the people who work for you, as well as treating them in a dignified manner. Businesses that practice TGR as a management principle tend to prosper.

Chapter 4 — Customer Disservice

A Customer's Rant

I hate it when you don't show up on time. I hate it when you're slow in returning my phone calls. I hate it when you point fingers at someone else every time there's a screw-up. I hate it when I have to pay you more than I expected.

I don't care how valuable your products and services may be or what you did for me last time, business is business. As long as I'm paying for your services, I'm the boss and you are my servant. I hate it when you act like you are the one doing me a favor instead of the other way around.

You see, I am The Customer. Each transaction makes me king of my tiny domain of commerce. I expect — no, make that DEMAND — to be treated not only with respect, but with indulgence. Always keep in mind that I don't have to do business with you. I have my choice of dozens, even hundreds of companies that can do the same thing you do and just as well, more or less.

For the most part, I don't give a hoot who I buy from, as long as I get the best value for my money. I don't care how big you are, how many locations you have or what your stock trades for on Wall Street. All I care about is Numero Uno — how I get treated, the quality of the goods and services I buy, and how it all impacts my comfort and convenience. Plus, of course, how much I have to pay.

It's none of your business, but I don't mind sharing that I am intoxicated with power. I love being The Customer. My wife may nag me, the kids may not listen to me, the boss may be on my back, but as long as I control some almighty bucks, I am a person with authority. Money is power. It enables me to distribute or withhold my favors as I see fit. It entitles me to give guff rather than take it.

Most of you don't see things my way. You do business based on your schedule, your needs, your temperament. That's why you're all so rich, huh?

I love having so many businesses to choose from. I love rewarding the ones that jump through hoops for me, and dismissing those who don't. Yessirree, I love being The Customer.

If you know what's good for you, you'll look beyond this obnoxious rant and learn to love me too.

Time For A Manners Check

The late 1990s were the best times ever for the airline industry. Seats were packed elbow-to-elbow and the airlines made more money than ever before. United Airlines, then the nation's biggest carrier, saw its stock price jet to more than $125 a share.

United's biggest hub is in my hometown of Chicago. They go almost everywhere out of O'Hare Airport and their fares back in those days were usually among the lowest, so I flew them a lot. (Plus, I was sucked in by their frequent flyer program,)

What I remember most about traveling in that prosperous era was the rudeness and arrogance of United employees. Years earlier United pilots had cut a deal with the company to forego some pay raises in return for a slice of ownership of the airline. Once business heated up, they decided they wanted more pay after all, in addition to owning a piece of the pie. When management didn't give them their way, the pilots engaged in sickouts and slowdowns, leading to an epidemic of flight delays and cancellations. This attitude reverberated throughout the company. Ticket agents, flight attendants and reservations staff all did their jobs with chips on their shoulder. Smiling faces were as rare as tasty meals in coach. With the airline booking almost all available seats, United employees felt free to treat passengers like nuisances.

Then divine justice intervened -- or at least that's one interpretation. United took a nosedive and ended up in bankruptcy. Thousands of employees lost their jobs and almost all who remained endured steep pay cuts. Stockholders – including many United employees who invested through the company's 401(k) plan – saw the value of their shares decline from triple figures to a big fat zero.

Something interesting coincided with these events. Flyers suddenly saw smiling faces everywhere at United. People desperate to hold onto their jobs got the message that it was good business to be nice to paying customers.

Counter-cyclical manners

Plenty of businesses fall into this pattern. When business revs up, business manners tend to head in the opposite direction.

That's when people get too busy to return customer calls. Complaints get ignored or challenged. Everyone is pushing hard and tempers get short. So what, many business owners think either consciously or subconsciously. There's more where they came from.

When business is booming, it's easy to delude yourself into thinking that customers need you more than you need them; that you are doing them a favor by doing the work they pay you to do or selling them merchandise they need.

When times are good, you can even get away with it for a while. It sure feels good to fire whining customers and tell them, "Who needs your guff. Take your business elsewhere."

Problem is, business cycles come and go. The rising tide that raises all ships can recede like seaside water before a tsunami. The Great Recession and stagnation of the late 2000s taught many companies that all of those customers who were mistreated during the boom times have long memories.

A Wall Street Journal article from June 7, 2010, "Customer Service as a Growth Engine,"described efforts by large organizations such as Walgreen's, Comcast, American Express and others to pay "more attention to customer service in an effort to increase sales and gain market share in the economic recovery." The Journal cited a survey of more than 1,400 companies that found more than a quarter saying customer service would be the prime target of increased funding once the economy improved.

To which I silently responded, DUH!

I wonder if it occurred to executives at all those companies surveyed that had they had paid more attention to customer service activities when the downturn hit, they might already be enjoying increased sales and market share. It's a real simple concept. People like to do business with companies that make it likeable to do business with them.

Yesterday you were the hammer, but today you're the nail. When the phones slow down you find yourself wanting to talk to the people whose calls you were too busy to return before. You also wish you had given them reason to recommend you to other people.

Friendliness comes easy

Customer service is not rocket science. You may struggle with the intricate details of running a business. You may lack funding for your entrepreneurial dreams. Yet no matter what business you are in or what your financial situation, anyone has the ability to instill good customer manners. You and your people do not require any special technical aptitude or know-how to master the art of friendliness. You don't need to buy expensive tools and equipment, nor do you need to spend a lot of time and money on training programs or consultants.

A lot of it just has to do with The Golden Rule – treat others as you would like to be treated. Understand that kind words generate better results than harsh ones. Also remember that nobody ever wins an argument with a customer. The best that can happen is you'll prove yourself right. Then the customer will resent you because of it and take his business elsewhere. Is that a victory worth having?

A distributor of plumbing supplies once shared with me company research revealing what customers expected out of their inside salespeople. Three issues topped the list by a wide margin:

- Be readily available.
- Be eager to help and knowledgeable.
- Be responsive. Return phone calls and respond to back order status.

Isn't this pretty much what customers want from any business?

Another friend of mine from the plumbing supply business, Ed Felten, wrote a book titled, *The Art of Supervising & Motivating People*. In autographing my copy, he wrote the following inscription that is worth taking to heart: "People will forget what you say or do, but they never forget how you made them feel."

Rudeness stems from something dark within the human soul. Don't succumb to it.

Four Customer Service Truths
That Can Make Or Break You

TARP was a business consulting firm based in Arlington, VA that specialized in customer experience research. Its clients included many of the nation's most recognizable Fortune 500 firms, as well as the federal government.

Back in 1999, TARP did some studies on customer satisfaction that stand as landmarks in the business world for analyzing customer behavior. Every business owner would do well to heed these four customer service truths uncovered by TARP's research.

Customer Service Truth #1: *Word of mouth is the best form of advertising.*

TARP's studies have shown that if you excel at customer service, each satisfied customer will tell an average of *three* other people about you.

This is encouraging. Think of it as getting three satisfied customers every time you excel at serving one.

However, before you get too excited about this, ponder for a moment the next profound truth, which ought to send a big chill up your spine.

Customer Service Truth #2: *Bad news travels further than good news.*

TARP also determined that if you mess up, each dissatisfied

customer will tell, on average, 15 other people about you!

Contemplate that arithmetic. If you do well by someone, that person will spread the word to three other people. But if you goof up, on average 15 other people will hear about it.

This means that you have to recruit *five* satisfied customers to make up for every one that gets peeved at you for whatever reason.

What's more, it is much easier to irritate someone in the course of doing business than to please a person, wouldn't you agree? Show up on time, do a decent job, charge a reasonable price, and most of the time you won't get any special thanks. That's what a customer had the right to expect all along, isn't it?

But inadvertently supply the wrong merchandise, say the wrong thing, take a little longer or charge a little more than expected, and you've made an enemy. If the customer is in a bad mood to begin with, the slightest misstep could trigger a snit fit.

This is the most daunting customer service truth. You have to truly excel at customer service to overcome all the badmouthing that is bound to come your way even when you try to do a good job.

How do you excel at service? By making it a high priority with everybody you employ. By recruiting not only competent workers, but "people" people who know how to interact with the public. Be sure to emphasize customer service and give some training to everyone in a job that involves customer contact.

Customer Service Truth #3: *Complainers are your best friends.*

TARP found that for every complaint made to a company, there are 26 silent, dissatisfied customers. Only 4% of customers with a grievance will bother to raise it with company personnel.

Think about this for a moment. For most people in business, dealing with complaints is the most agonizing part of their work. Actually, you ought to cherish the complainers. Their complaints serve the same purpose as a baby's cry. The 4% who tell you they're ticked off are the ones who inform you that something is wrong, and thus give you a chance to correct it. The 96% who suffer in silence are the ones you have to worry about. They simply go to a competitor without ever giving you a chance to make amends.

Customer Service Truth #4: *Customer anger can be turned to your advantage.*

Of customers who do complain and receive a satisfactory response, TARP found that 70% become a firm's most loyal customers.

Just as reformed sinners become the most avid churchgoers, so it is with customers who get turned around. A mistake is an opportunity to solidify business relationships and establish long-term bonds. It enables you to talk at length to a person as you investigate the complaint. This helps you get to know them, to connect with them as a friend.

Learn to love the complainers.

Failures To Communicate

"Communication failure" is a catch-all term that leads to many business migraines. Failures to communicate happen in many ways, for many reasons. Let's examine some of these, and what can be done to correct them.

- **"It's not my responsibility."**

Or, "It's not my department … It's not my job." Worst of all, is when it doesn't get stated at all. Someone who works for you hears a request or a complaint from a customer, but simply shrugs it off. After all, his job is to make sure all paperwork is shuffled correctly, not deal with whiny grouches!

As a boss, you must take responsibility for such attitudes. It stems from failure to instill customer service and satisfaction as part of everyone's job description. If you're a company's chief financial officer you're unlikely to have much customer contact, but if you ever encounter one by accident you'd better be prepared to treat them like your boss. Ditto if you drive a forklift in the warehouse, or hang out in a cubicle keeping the books.

Customer service & satisfaction is every employee's responsibility.

That's not a bad slogan to post where everyone can see it. Not everyone has it in his/her power to correct the problem a customer brings up. But everyone must be expected to listen, understand and direct the customer towards a solution. Don't tell the customer to contact someone in another department. *You* contact the relevant person and let them know there is a customer in urgent need of assistance.

- **"I assumed …"**

It's such common knowledge, we can assume everyone knows it, right? For example, everyone in my line of work knows what the expression "spike a story" refers to. It means to kill it, and derives from the old days when copy editors literally had an upward raised spike on their desks where they would skewer manuscripts they didn't intend to use.

Oh, you didn't know that? But it's common knowledge among all the people I worked with. I just assumed you knew!

People from different walks of life carry around a body of knowledge familiar to everyone in their field. When you spend most of your waking hours hanging around working colleagues, it becomes second nature to naturally assume the person you're dealing with understands the same "inside baseball" talk that you're used to.

No doubt there are a thousand details about your business that I don't have a clue about. I run into this all the time when I interview business people and they start throwing around jargon and acronyms that are second nature to them but Greek to me. It becomes tedious at times asking them to clarify terms, and I'm sure some of them must think I'm dumb as a rock for not knowing that stuff. Yet I feel compelled to ask questions until I'm confident I understand what's going on. That's what good journalists are supposed to do.

Except most people aren't professional journalists. They won't do that. They will pretend to understand out of fear of being considered stupid. And that's how assumptions can turn into a costly failure to communicate.

- **"I think so."**

I roll my eyes every time some customer service rep tells me, "I think the order was shipped … I'm pretty sure your request was passed along." My knee-jerk response is to ask: "Which is it, do you *think* you know or do you know? … Are you *pretty sure*, or are you certain?"

What's behind this is simply laziness. People are under the impression that something was done, but won't make an effort to take whatever steps are necessary to verify that it was.

Think about how many times you thought something had been taken care of but it had not. When in doubt, double-check.

- **If it's not in writing, it's not real.**

This may be the most common failure to communicate. You say something, maybe more than once, perhaps over and over, so you just have to "assume" – there's that word again – that everyone gets it. Not so.

I spent some time heading my condo association's communications committee, and I recall a time when the president was lamenting the fact that she had to keep repeating so much of the same information over and over at our meetings. Of course you do, I told her, because verbal information tends to go in one ear and out the other. Or it gets mixed up with other information. People have selective memories and tend to hear what they want to hear. Plus, not everyone attends every meeting. That's why it's important to publish a regular newsletter, of which I served as editor.

Same goes for all of the information you transmit to company associates. Don't expect much of it to register via casual conversation. It has to be put in writing.

Even that isn't enough. Once put in writing, the documentation has to be posted and/or disseminated in thorough and timely fashion. Policy statements buried in an employee manual won't do much good if they are not reinforced via bulletin boards, memos, etc.

- **Lack of follow through.**

Once I was invited to be a speaker at a trade group's luncheon scheduled for a date in November, or so I was originally told. I reserved the date on my calendar, and even had to rearrange some other business travel to accommodate it. I heard nothing from the party who invited me until early October, when I received a fax transmission reminding me of the *October 11* luncheon meeting. To make matters worse, the subject line on the fax still made reference to the "November meeting."

Whoa! I got on the phone and never could reach the executive director of the trade group, who had invited me. He had everything filtered through an administrative assistant, who knew nothing other than what she was instructed to type and fax to me. She couldn't tell me if the meeting was to be held on the October date or in November. To make matters worse, I had a schedule conflict on the October 11 date.

It took several phone calls to straighten things out, mainly because the staff chief kept communicating through his assistant, who did not have enough information. I finally told her that I simply wouldn't show up unless I heard from her boss within 24 hours. Only then did he call me. He was duly apologetic and said the meeting was for the October date after all – and pretty much begged me to rearrange my schedule, because a large audience was expected.

I gave in, because my other appointment for that date was easily changed, but I let him know how unhappy I was at the poor communications.

His failures to communicate included 1. failing to follow through with me in timely fashion; 2. failing to communicate not only with me, but with his assistant; 3. failing to take charge even when it was clear that something went wrong.

The business world is filled with snafus like this that waste time and convey an image of disorganization. It's why people show up for appointments that have been rescheduled, or fail to show up for the same reason. It's why job quotes and materials requisitions get sidetracked for months because nobody thinks to follow up on them; people forget about verbal commitments because nobody put it in writing.

Make it a point to confirm deadlines and appointments as the dates draw near. Make sure everyone is on the same page with who, what, where and when.

- **Imprecise communication.**

A message came to me through the website of a magazine of which I was editor. "Can't find any info on your website about copyright policies. Please explain."

Beats me what he means by that. I *assume* (uh oh) he would like permission to reprint something that appeared in the magazine, but if that's the case, why didn't he just come right out and tell me what it was he wanted permission to use.

Imprecise communication stems from fuzzy thinking, and fuzzy thinking sometimes stems from inarticulateness, i.e., people just can't think of the right words to express themselves. It's not a problem associated only with folks of limited vocabulary. My world of wordsmiths is filled with people who have degrees in journalism and English, but who nonetheless have trouble communicating exactly what they want. Government agency staffers have invented a language of their own known as "bureaucratese" that defies interpretation by the average citizen.

Vagueness and impenetrable lingo waste time. Instead of communicating something once, they cause both the sender and recipient of the message to read and re-read, and maybe follow up with personal contact to try to clarify what's going on

Even worse, they'll be too lazy to clarify, and simply act upon what they *think* the request is about, what they *assume* is being asked for.

So many ways to fail to communicate. So many times it happens.

I'm a big fan of "management by walking around," which is as described. Certain bosses make it a point to schedule time to simply observe operations, ask questions, listen to complaints and comments, and witness how employees are dealing with customers in both casual and unusual encounters. Good advice.

Mind Your Telephone Manners

I was in a bad mood when I wrote this section, which made it a good time to address a pet peeve. The reason for my bad mood was a phone call I had just made — three phone calls, actually — trying to reschedule an annual appointment with my ophthalmologist. My eye doctor is highly regarded but I can't say the same for his receptionist, who put me on hold three times during our conversation, the first time even before I had a chance to identify myself:

"Dr. Eyeball's office, please hold." (Doesn't it drive you up a wall when you get rejected even before you get a chance to say your name?)

The second time was a few seconds into our conversation after she picked up the line again. I had enough time to tell her my name, but not the purpose of my call, when she put me on hold again without asking my permission. There I stewed for perhaps 20 seconds, though it always feels like 20 minutes.

Third time it happened, I hung up, then redialed. Soon as she answered, I told her I'm tired of being put on hold, gave her my preferred date for a new appointment, and left my number for her to call me back when she could confirm a booking for that date. She started to get sassy, but I cut her short saying that the time it took to argue with me could be better spent rebooking my appointment. I then suggested she ask the Doc to send her to a class on customer service and telephone etiquette — "Or would you prefer that I tell him?" I asked.

She called back shortly afterward with a new date, and an apologetic tone. I take no pleasure in haranguing telephone receptionists, yet I'm sorry to say it sometimes gets results.

It shouldn't be necessary. I understand that sometimes things do get hectic. Nonetheless, whether you are in the doctoring business or any other kind, there are techniques for handling multiple incoming calls that don't try the patience of a caller.

Actually, the office had a solution already in hand, though they made poor use of it. I actually made three phone calls into the ophthalmologist's office. The first call reached a voice message system, which stated the office hours and said that if I reached this message during those hours, it was because both phone lines were tied up and to call back later, which I did.

Almost a good solution. Even better would be a message inviting me to leave my number, with a promise to call me back as soon as the office staff had a free moment. The dentist I patronize has a system like that, and I appreciate the fact that it shows consideration for the patient/customer.

The Most Important Person In Your Company

That's what my friend Dan Holohan called telephone receptionists. Dan is one of the country's top heating consultants, specializing in hydronic ("wet") heating systems (www.heatinghelp.com), but he is equally proficient as a business and marketing analyst. Dan has authored numerous books, of which my personal favorite is *Just Add H2Oh! (A Recipe for Hydronic Marketing Success)*. Here's an excerpt:

"I think the most important person in your company is the person who first answers your telephone. You know why this person is so important? Because this is the first person the customer talks to. This person is more important to your company than any salesperson, manager, technician, installer, or even the owner because *nothing* happens until someone answers the phone.

"Most one- or two-person shops use answering services. If you use one of these, call them frequently and see how long it takes for them to pick up. Listen to what they say when they do pick up. I have a friend who once used a service that was based 1,000 miles away from his office …

"The person answering his phone had a back-woods southern accent that sounded like a mixture of Jack Daniels and pork bellies. She couldn't pronounce his very ethnic name. She'd try two or three times when she picked up the call, and then finally wing it. She never said it the same way twice. She was talking mostly to people from New York who have their own troubles speaking English. It was a disaster.

"But he got a good price.

"If you use an answering service, have friends call and pretend they're potential customers. See how the service treats them. This could be one of the best things you ever do because nothing happens until that phone rings. And the one who answers that phone is the most important person in your company."

Dan wrote that book back in 1997 and it's a bit dated in that answering services have largely been replaced by automated voice messaging systems even in small companies. But his observation about the importance of first customer contact remains right on the money.

What's at stake

Home repair firms are particularly in need of top-notch telephone manners. Over the years I have blown off countless home repair contractors whose initial contact gave the impression of an amateurish operation. Could be some of them were the best in their business when it came to trade work, though I doubt it. Business owners who are lackadaisical about telephone reception probably have other shortcomings, to my way of thinking.

Telephone receptionists often are the lowest-paid employees in an organization. In small companies often this not a job unto itself but a secondary duty of office staffers who get annoyed at phone calls that interrupt their main chores. Their voices betray that aggravation. They may not even realize they're being impolite, except what counts is the perception of the caller.

The person who answers your phone is like the leadoff batter in baseball. A team is much more likely to score when the leadoff man gets a hit than when he strikes out. Likewise, the person who answers your phone creates a first impression that can make or break business opportunities.

Answering a business telephone isn't brain surgery. It doesn't require extraordinary credentials or top pay. Still, whoever does the job ought to receive more than cursory training on what to say, guidelines for handling multiple incoming calls, dealing with irate callers, forwarding calls and so on.

Unlike most business problems, solutions to this one are simple and cheap. It merely takes a little instruction in proper telephone and customer service techniques. Here are some of the deficiencies I routinely notice and how to correct them.

- **Consider an automated phone answering system.**

Automated voice messaging has eliminated the need for phone receptionists in many companies. Some people may still yearn to speak with a live person but by now are used to automated systems and shrug off the impersonality.

Automated messaging is better than an incompetent live receptionist, as long as the messages are brief and the button presses limited. Nobody likes to deal with endless menu instructions, but it's mostly large companies that have the complex systems. Smaller companies can get by with simpler menu options.

One should always be, "Press zero to speak with a live operator."

- **Minimize on-hold.**

If you must put callers on-hold, make it a point to keep them on no longer than 30 seconds at a time. Studies have shown that most callers will hang up after 30 seconds on hold. If the caller cannot be serviced within 30 seconds, before that time has passed get back on the line and say: "I'm sorry, but it's taking a little longer than expected. Would you prefer to keep holding, or can someone call you back?"

- **It's not only what you say, but how you say it.**

Face it, answering the phone all day is not the world's most exciting job. Too often this boredom comes through in the receptionist's tone of voice. Even worse, some receptionists convey the feeling they're annoyed by the call, as if it's interrupting more pressing business — like a boyfriend on the other line.

Academic research has uncovered what's become known as the 7-38-55 rule. That is, words account for 7% of the message communicated, tone of voice 38% and body language 55%. This means customers react to your posture and tone much more than what you're actually saying. If you're dealing with someone in person, you can say all the right things but still appear untrustworthy if you're frowning and failing to make eye contact.

In person or on the phone, it's important to sound chipper at all times. A smile on one's face forces people to sound upbeat. A favorite trick of telemarketers and professional customer service reps is to keep a mirror by the phone at all times. They practice that smile as they speak. Not a bad idea for anyone whose job requires a lot of phone contact.

- **Clipped responses.**

Often I hear, "He's not in right now." Then silence. Inquiries often get answered with clipped responses such as: "I don't know ... I'm afraid I can't help you ... We don't do that." Abrupt responses like this come across as grouchy and grate on a caller's nerves. They need to be replaced by, "I don't know, but I'll try to put you in touch with someone who does."

Everyone who answers the phone for a business must understand that their job is not only to answer the phone but to assist callers in getting to the right person or obtaining the right information. It's like military basic training, which teaches every soldier rudimentary combat skills. Similarly, every employee needs basic customer service skills.

- **Screening vs. welcoming.**

In many companies phone receptionists are trained to ask the purpose of a call in order to deflect pesky salesmen. This is understandable. Business owners and managers are too busy to be listening to unwanted sales pitches all day long.

At the same time phone receptionists are expected to extend a warm welcome to potential customers or VIPs. A natural tug-of-war exists between these conflicting functions. Is there any foolproof way to screen out the pests without alienating important callers? Probably not. So, instruct your receptionists to treat everyone politely, and if there's any doubt, put the call through. The worst you can lose is a few seconds of time. The worst that can happen when putting off a legitimate customer or prospect is losing a lifetime worth of business.

- **Steps for dealing with angry callers.**

1. Listen carefully. Be sure to understand the nature of the complaint.

2. Pause before responding. Never interrupt. When you do speak, say something like, "I understand your frustration. Let me help."

3. If anger turns to abuse, say, "Taking it out on me will not solve your problem. Please give me a chance to help you."

4. Avoid the word "you," as in, "You need to ..." Instead, say things like "I would recommend, or "May I suggest."

- **Top phone receptionists make every effort to ...**

— Answer every call on the first ring.

— Tell the caller the name of the person and extension number when transferring, just in case of a disconnect.

— Ask callers if it's okay to put them on hold before doing so.

-- Let the caller hang up first to guard against an abrupt, premature cutoff.

Chapter 5 – It's About Time

Workaholism Is A Disease

For a business owner or top manager there never seem to be enough hours in the day. I noted in the first chapter that when you choose to start your own business you can expect to put in grueling hours. The minimum is about 60 hours per week, and that can easily rise to 70-80 during peak periods or when an emergency arises.

I've encountered many business people who routinely work that many hours in a week or more. Some like to describe themselves as workaholics and claim to thrive spending all that time on the job. To me, one of two things is wrong with them.

First is that, if they are genuine workaholics, they need to realize that workaholism is more a vice than a virtue. It's an affliction just like alcoholism or drug addiction.

While it's good to have a strong work ethic, it's even more important to enjoy life and provide not only monetary but also emotional support to your loved ones. Small business owners miss out on many family activities. The kids are already in bed by the time many of them return home from them daily toil, and sometimes when they are at home they're mired in paperwork or on the phone tending to business. Workaholism is not a virtue when it causes you to miss too many of life's most precious moments.

Second point is, more often than not, workaholism is not voluntary. Business owners and managers who put in overly long hours tend to describe themselves as workaholics when the real issue is they don't know how to manage their time. They work hard rather than smart. They fail to delegate. They are in a vicious cycle in which they are so busy they have no time to plan and organize their work, and failing to plan and organize guarantees they will always be busy in an unproductive way.

Results are what count

Hard work wins no prizes. Results are what count, and long hours do not necessarily correlate with superior performance. A large body of evidence suggests that the opposite holds true.

A study commissioned some years ago by the investment firm Charles Schwab & Co. found that investment advisors who put in 60 hours a week or more on average generated less income per hour than those who worked the industry average of 45 to 50 hours. The study found that fatigue, both physical and mental, drains away productivity. Similar studies have been done on manual workers who put in overtime and almost all have found that productivity diminishes during overtime hours.

Parkinson's Law also comes into play. This is named after a British economist who famously observed that "work expands to fill the time available." If a Herculean workweek becomes the norm, you'll find plenty of things to do to fill the time, even though the essential work could be fitted into fewer hours.

My wife once worked for a large Japanese-owned corporation that had an American president and other Americans in key operational positions. Sprinkled among them were a CEO and a handful of middle managers from Japan. It was a high-pressure business environment in which everyone put in more than 40 hours a week, but the Japanese were culturally conditioned to hang around later at night than the Americans. None of the Japanese staffers wanted to turn off their lights until the Japanese CEO finally decided to call it a day. Then a chain reaction of underlings would rapidly follow him out the door. The value of their output was nowhere near commensurate with the time these salarymen put in, however. Mostly they generated an endless stream of useless reports, but their culture compelled them to stay late and look busy.

Peer pressure works on American workers as well as Japanese, although maybe to a lesser degree. In many businesses the perception is widespread that difficult jobs require extended working hours. People who arrive and leave on time get labeled as "clock watchers."

A corollary to Parkinson's Law is that there will never be enough time to do everything that human ingenuity can concoct in running a business. You can think up endless projects that seem like good ideas. You must choose which ones are most important, feasible and worth the time and effort.

A man I knew who owned one of the largest trade service firms in the country was to me a quintessential workaholic. I'd written a couple of stories about his company and spent many hours in conversation with him over the years – always about business. Sometimes he'd wear me out talking shop and I'd try turning the conversation to sports, global affairs or anything else just to reboot our minds, but to no avail. He seemed to have no interest in anything except his business. Although this entrepreneur came up with brilliant innovations and built a wildly successful company, some of his ideas were over the top. For instance, he spent years trying to perfect a system for taking inventory of little parts by weighing the bins containing them. Conversations I had with him about the subject led me to believe he must've invested way too many hours on this project but the counts never were precise enough for him.

I always thought, what's the point? The little pieces he was concerned about cost a few dimes each, and even if he lost track of hundreds of them each month it would amount to a fly speck marring his bottom line. In fact, he seemed more interested in the challenge of devising a weighing system than in saving money. Such are the ways of workaholics.

For the sake of your own mental and physical health, those of you who put in monumental hours on the job need to focus on cutting back. This requires delegating some responsibilities and managing time more effectively.

Take control of your job

Anyone who runs a business is never in total control over the workload and the time it takes to perform all tasks. You cannot predict how many customers will call on any given day, what services they may require, how urgent those services may be, or how much time it will take to solve their problems.

On certain days you may find yourself spending virtually all your time troubleshooting emergencies. These situations will throw anyone's day plan out of whack. At times you may feel frustrated at not being able to finish everything you intended to do. On these days you may well have to burn the proverbial midnight oil to satisfy customers and keep your business running smoothly.

Most days, however, you'll find to be fairly routine and predictable. You must take control of your business and your job by planning and managing the time you devote to routine duties. This will enable you to tend to urgent and unanticipated tasks without sacrificing overall job performance.

Time management is largely a matter of setting priorities. You want to spend the most time on those tasks that are most important.

Nothing is more important than time spent talking to customers. When a customer comes in to your place of business or places a phone call, that customer deserves your full attention. It's time to put aside paperwork, e-mail and other tasks that can be done later.

Every customer conversation can be regarded as a sales call. That's because every customer contact helps to shape that customer's attitude toward you and your business. How you handle these discussions will set the stage for sales over time.

If the customer has a problem, it's an opportunity for you to solve it. If s/he requests information, the speed and thoroughness of your response will determine how much confidence the customer places in you. Customer conversations allow you opportunities to help customers and learn more about their wants and needs.

You want to maximize sales opportunities. That's why no duties should have a higher priority than customer contact.

16 Top Time Wasters

After you put customers on their proper pedestal, it's time to identify and eliminate the biggest time wasters in your business. Here are some notorious time wasters.

1. Mistakes.

Haste makes waste. If you take a few extra seconds to do something right, you can save hours of time wasted doing it all over again. Correcting mistakes and dealing with the problems they cause are the biggest time wasters in a company. I've seen studies showing that salespeople spend about a quarter of their working hours dealing with problems and mistakes.

The basic premise of this book has to do with the mistakes that kill small businesses. The next three chapters are devoted to mistakes and how to eliminate them.

2. Lack of delegation.

Entrepreneurs often have trouble with delegation. Hard-driven, hard-working individuals usually fail to trust any associates to complete tasks as well as they can do it themselves. A common refrain is: "I can do it myself a lot faster than I can teach someone else to do it."

This may be true, but only the first time for a given task. Too often the boss takes it upon himself to perform routine tasks time after time that could be adequately performed by lower paid (and less busy) assistants.

Here's a mantra for any business owner to follow as pertains to job delegation and time management:

Assign every task to the lowest-paid employee capable of performing that task acceptably.

Some tasks, like setting strategic direction or dealing with VIP customers, should only be performed by the owner or a top manager. Middle managers and field workers may be capable of handling many other important day-to-day business chores, while some necessary but fairly uncomplicated tasks can be delegated all the way down to a receptionist or mail clerk.

3. Needless business tasks.

Some tasks seem important but really do nothing but waste time. Like second guessing an associate's way of doing something. Or handling the same piece of paper two or three times. Or performing tasks normally assigned to an administrative assistant. Unless you run a one-person operation, don't try to do everything yourself.

Also keep in mind that not every task needs to be done every day. And some duties are more important than others.

You'll find that business tasks follow Paredo's Law. More commonly known as the "80/20" rule, Paredo's Law refers to a curious natural phenomenon that many human endeavors tend to follow an approximate 80/20 ratio. For instance, most businesses find that about 80% of sales revenues come from around 20% of their customers. Paredo's Law also determines that about 80% of your time should be spent on about 20% of your most important duties.

We've already identified one of the most important duties – customer contact. If you find yourself spending close to 80% of your time dealing with customers, pat yourself on the back!

4. Pointless meetings.

Yes, some staff meetings serve useful purposes as brainstorming sessions and pulling together as a team. They are also a handy way to disseminate important information to a large number of people at once. Yet, for every one that fulfills those useful functions better than alternative ways to communicate, dozens end up as nothing more than meandering, useless discussions.

Nonproductive meetings have been a pet peeve of mine throughout my career. Between work and various volunteer organizations that I've belonged to, too many days of my life have been frittered away in bull sessions that accomplished little or nothing. Countless times I've walked away from a meeting muttering to myself about what a waste of time that was. I'm sure all of you have had the same experience.

The good news is that the need for staff meetings is diminishing, thanks to e-mail. Probably 90% of the information that needs to be conveyed to people you work with can be better done electronically rather than in face-to-face group encounters.

Advantages of e-mail over meetings are plentiful:

- E-mail documents who said what and who's responsible for certain tasks.
- You can copy as many or as few people as necessary. Persons not copied generally don't know they've been excluded, which avoids the hurt feelings and office politics that result when certain individuals get excluded from group meetings.
- E-mail is much, much quicker and encourages to-the-point brevity.
- You can send or read e-mail any time of night and day.
- Participants need not disrupt their work to be present at a specific time and place.

E-mail also has a few disadvantages. Some people communicate better verbally than with the written word, so people who are not good writers but full of good ideas may not get a fair hearing via e-mail. Moreover, e-mail misses the body language and voice inflections that are so important to communication.

So, meetings are here to stay. The goal should be to minimize them and make those that do take place as productive as possible. Here are some tips to achieve those objectives.

- **Don't be afraid to cancel regularly scheduled meetings**.

Monday morning staff meetings are a hoary tradition in the business world. They're aimed at making plans for the coming week and reviewing progress made the previous week. But the problem with regularly scheduled meetings is the meetings become ends unto themselves. Participants get in the habit of meeting because they're supposed to have a meeting, whether or not there is anything important to be discussed. If you feel time could be better spent elsewhere, don't hesitate to cancel a meeting. Better yet, don't have regularly scheduled meetings, only those called ad hoc to deal with specific issues.

- **Meetings need a written agenda.**

A meeting without an agenda is a bull session. Sometimes great ideas come out of bull sessions. But B.S. can take place during lunch breaks, over cocktails, on the golf course, in fishing boats, or wherever else colleagues may gather on their own time. B.S. has no place during business hours. If you are going to occupy the time of people on your payroll while the meter is running, it needs to be for the purpose of discussing specific business issues. That requires a meeting, not a bull session.

And a meeting requires an agenda. It should outline the topics for discussion at the meeting — the more specific the better. You cannot address "business problems" in a one-hour meeting. There's only enough time to address one or two specific problems, like "collections" or "tardiness," or "let's eliminate meetings."

- **Put a time limit on every meeting**.

Agendas should have time limits assigned to each item on the agenda, and the meeting itself should have a time limit. This would vary, of course, with the scope of the meeting, but you're kidding yourself if you think you'll resolve three times as many issues in a three-hour meeting as you would in a one-hour session. People wear out. Discussions go off on tangents. Bathroom breaks become necessary. Keep meetings as short as possible.

Here's another tip: time meetings to end at quitting time. It will reduce the temptation for people to prattle on and extend the meeting.

- **Dictators run the best meetings.**

A tight agenda and time limits are useless without a dictator to enforce them. Whoever presides over a meeting must be ruthless in keeping to the agenda and to the time limits. This person ought to verge on rudeness in cutting off speakers who ramble.

If nobody volunteers, the meeting leader needs to assign specific tasks to specific individuals, along with deadlines for completion. If a discussion topic runs past its time limit, the meeting chairperson needs to decide whether to cut off discussion, or continue it and table something else on the agenda for a later time.

Without a dictator presiding, meetings always degenerate into bull sessions. Always.

- **Productive meetings require defined objectives.**

What is the purpose of any given meeting and what is the expected outcome? If you can't give a pointed answer to these questions, don't bother holding a meeting. A single objective is best. Some good reasons to hold a meeting include informing large numbers of people of something they all have a stake in, brainstorming a proposal, organizing a project and assigning responsibilities. Meetings may also function as training sessions, or to dispel a rumor or break some news, good or bad.

Just be sure the defined objective isn't to hold a meeting!

- **Consider stand-up meetings.**

This is becoming popular within some organizations. You gather in a room without chairs and maybe even without tables. While standing you discuss whatever needs to be discussed. People quickly tire of standing so the meetings tend to be short and to the point. This might be a good alternative for those Monday morning sessions just to get everyone on the same page.

- **Someone needs to take notes and disseminate them – within 24 hours.**

Without a written record the same issues will get debated In meeting after meeting without resolution. That's when people say, "Didn't we cover that already?" while everyone scratches their heads in vague recollection. Moreover, everyone has selective memory. We tend to remember discussions that went to our liking, while forgetting those that didn't. Also, note-taking assures that specific individuals are held accountable for tasks assigned.

Copies of the meeting notes should be sent to all meeting participants, with names listed so everyone has a record of who was present—along with the time and date of the meeting. Do this the same day of the meeting or no later than the next day while recall is fresh and people are still focused on the subjects discussed.

The recorder should invite anyone who disputes a point in the notes to take it up with the recorder within a reasonable deadline. If someone disputes the notes, revised notes may be necessary—again, disseminated to all participants. If nobody objects, then the notes stand as an accurate record of that meeting.

Does this sound like a lot of trouble to go through? It is. If the meeting isn't important enough to go through all this rigmarole, then the meeting is unnecessary.

- **Calculate the cost of a meeting.**

Break down the hourly pay of each participant. Add the total and multiply by the hours or fraction thereof taken up by the meeting.

You'll find that most staff meetings cost more than $1,000 when you factor in the value of peoples' time. Ask yourself whether the results of that meeting were worth the cost. Don't spend your hard-earned money on bull sessions.

5. Procrastination.

Another business time waster is putting off unpleasant tasks. That means it comes up for discussion or analysis multiple times. Your mind will be free and uncluttered if you make it a point to get unpleasantries out of the way quickly.

Procrastination often results from indecision. You don't quite know how to handle a situation, so you put it aside to think it over … and over … and over …

If you don't know how to handle something, seek advice from trusted friends and business colleagues. Then take care of it and get it out of the way.

Another aspect of procrastination is that certain individuals get a rush from putting things off till the last minute. They think they work best when meeting deadlines by the narrowest of margins. These same people tend to habitually show up late for appointments or with seconds to spare. I've worked with many people like that throughout my career, and I have to concede that some of them were effective performers.

I can't say for sure whether their clock-ticking dramas helped them be effective or whether they succeeded in spite of that behavior. What I can say with certainty is that it annoyed the heck of out me and many other colleagues.

6. Misuse of computers.

For the most part computers are time-saving tools that have boosted productivity throughout the business world. Yet just as evil can be considered the flip side of good, computers can hamper productivity via excessive internet surfing and incessant checking of email. Make it a terminable offense if people use company computers to visit porn or gambling websites.

Computers also get misused when they spit out endless reports of useless or, worse, misleading information that takes time to read and analyze.

7. Poor rhythm.

Working days in every field have an ebb and flow of busy and slow periods. Identify the rhythm of your typical workday and schedule activities accordingly.

If there are certain times of day when customer visits or phone calls stack up, make it a point to clear your desk and make yourself available to customers at those times. If the phones typically don't start heating up till mid-morning, then devote the early morning hours to paperwork, e-mail, etc. If slack time tends to come in the afternoon, then schedule your paperwork at those times.

Another aspect to the working day rhythm is your own tempo. Some people are morning folks while others don't really get their bodies and minds revved up till later in the day. For instance, I've always been a morning person when it comes to creativity, so I tried to arrive at the office early and do as much writing as possible in the a.m. hours. My administrative duties were best relegated to the afternoon.

8. Wasting customers' time.

Worse than wasting your own time is when you drag customers into the same abyss. Your customers are busy just like you, and they resent the hell out of cold sales calls and conversations that meander around sports, weather and anything else except the business at hand. Learn your customers' schedules so as not to disturb them during their busy periods. Don't try to sell them products or services that are not a good fit. Learn their preferences and buying habits. Avoid wasting their time and yours, or you'll give them a reason to take a look at competing businesses.

9. Disorganization.

Keeping orderly files and a neat desk is more than a matter of appearance. It will help you save time. For every customer, you should have a folder containing all paperwork devoted to that customer – orders, notes of previous conversations, background information, maybe a printout of the customer's key web pages, etc. When the folder starts getting too thick, start a new one organized by year or some other parameter.

Bring out the folder and take a few moments to review it before contact with a customer. Have your filing system nearby for quick and easy retrieval in case a customer calls you. Keep the information in front of you when speaking to a customer.

Failure to think things through and plan activities can cost you a lot of time and energy. Planning ahead helps eliminate costly mistakes.

10. Urgent vs. vital.

Another time waster is failure to distinguish between the urgent and the vital. Years ago I would have encouraged you to distinguish between the urgent and the "trivial." In today's fast-paced business world, almost everything seems important.

So, let's get rid of the "trivial" concept. Instead think in terms of "urgent" versus "vital." A vital need for any business is to have a backup system in place in case of computer failure. An urgent situation would arise when the breakdown actually occurs.

Urgent requests call for immediate action. Vital tasks need to be done as soon as possible, but not necessarily this instant.

A daily "to do" list helps some people schedule their days. If you find this a helpful exercise, list them in order of priority. For instance, if there are 10 items on your daily "to do" list, it may be that only two of them are "urgent" – as opposed to "vital." In keeping with Paredo's Law, you may want to devote, say, six out of eight hours in your workday to these tasks. The other two hours would be devoted to the remaining eight tasks on the list.

Take advantage of modern electronics by using their calendars to schedule appointments and activities. It's quick, easy and handy to have your schedule available at a glance of your smart phone or iPad.

11. Clutter wastes time.

When a business owner or manager runs out of room in a desk and/or file cabinet, the typical response is to get a bigger desk or cabinet. In most cases, it's time to start tossing stuff out.

Clutter frequently results from hanging on to too much paperwork. This happens when people can't decide what to do with it. They'll keep a document on their desk or in a file because they are afraid it will turn out to be important, even if it doesn't seem to be at the moment they first read it. They waste time reading it over and over trying to determine what to do with it.

You'll save time if you make it a point to read every piece of paper that crosses your desk only once. Then, do one of three things with it: 1. Save it in an appropriate location; 2. Pass it on to someone else; 3. Throw it away.

Here are some questions to distinguish clutter from paperwork worth saving:

- Does this require action?
- Does it exist elsewhere?
- Would it be difficult to get again?
- Does it have legal implications?
- Is the information up to date?

If the answers are "yes" to the second question and "no" to the rest, ask one more question:

What's the worst thing that could happen if I didn't have this?

If you can live with the results, toss it.

I should practice what I preach. Years ago during my company's move to a different office building, I filled several dumpsters with old papers, magazines, research materials, etc. I estimate I threw out at least a ton of trash before moving to smaller quarters. In sorting through the materials, I noticed various documents that I had looked for in the past but couldn't find because I didn't remember where I filed them. Yes, I'm a pack rat, but do as I say, not as I do.

Clutter pertains to electronic files as well as paper files. Computer folders and files also tend to proliferate and become disorganized. You need a logical system for organizing computer files by customer, by brand, by time, by territory, or by any other parameters that may be relevant.

12. Inability to say no.

Be careful with this one. You want to be cooperative and assist employees and outsiders when they ask your help. Sometimes, though, certain individuals may ask you to do things that are unreasonable. It might be a time-consuming task that has nothing to do with your talents and duties.

Situations like this require a judgment call. If it's a good friend asking you to do a favor, maybe you'll say yes. Yet, the request might also come from a shirker just looking to pass off an unpleasant duty. Do you have time to do their job along with your own?

13. Multitasking.

Some people handle this better than others, and I'm hesitant to advise anyone not to handle two tasks at once, like signing routine documents while talking on the phone. However, in many cases it is a recipe for stress and mistakes, which are the biggest time wasters of all.

14. Relying on memory.

Some people have great memories – I count myself among them. Usually I have no trouble remembering appointments, phone numbers, etc. One thing I've learned over the years, however, is that my memorization is even more keen if I take time to jot something down. Even if I never again refer to my notes, the very act of writing it out helps reinforce the memory.

Plus, those jottings serve as backup data for those occasions when memory does fail, which it is bound to do with passage of time and information overload. Also, having things written down frees your mind for more creative thinking than trying to remember information.

15. Distractions.

Distractions are an enemy of time management and also inevitable. In the modern world of business the only way to completely avoid distractions is to set up shop in some remote cave in the desert. (The bats will drive a night shift crazy, however!)

Short of acquiring a Death Valley business address, there are some ways to minimize and manage the interruptions that attend every business day. The simplest way is to shut your door and not answer your phone when you need to concentrate on some important task. You can't become a business hermit, of course, but this falls into that category of distinguishing between urgent and vital tasks. For urgent duties requiring your full attention, tackle them without distractions.

16. Failure to take breaks.

This may seem counterintuitive, but I think failing to take breaks during the work day is a bigger time waster than taking 15 minutes or so off in segments throughout the day to let your mind and body reboot. Neither the human brain nor body is geared for peak performance working 10-12 hours straight, especially under stress.

Make it a point to take a lunch break each day. If you go out to lunch, try to go at off-peak hours, like 11:00 a.m. or 2:00 p.m. Wait staff won't be as busy and you'll get served quicker. If you're more into a sandwich at your desk, at least combine the meal with some nonbusiness reading, such as the daily newspaper. From time to time take five minutes off for a quick stroll, a cup of coffee or just to close the door and decompress at your desk. Make a phone call home or to a friend just to say hello and talk about pleasant personal experiences.

In the old comic books, Superman had the ability to manipulate the past and future by flying around the world at super-speed to increase or slow down the earth's rotation. That would be a marvelous way to add a few hours to the day. Alas, we are not Superman. All we can do is make best use of the business hours available to us by working smart and setting priorities.

Chapter 6 – Stop Shrugging Off Mistakes

No Margin For Error

"What are you waiting for?" my wife asked me.
"For the receipt," I replied.
"Why bother," she said.
"Don't you ever take a receipt when you get cash?"
"Nope," she replied. "The bank never makes a mistake."

That snippet of conversation took place at our bank's drive-through ATM, where I had pulled in to replenish pocket cash. Uh oh, was my first reaction. Jenny's casual attitude set off alarm bells in me over our household finances. Did we really have as much money in our accounts as we figured?

Except after thinking it over it dawned on me that she was right. We have made thousands of ATM transactions over the years since these machines turned up everywhere, and I can't recall a single mistake in the amount of cash dispensed or in the recordkeeping. Our checkbook doesn't always balance with our monthly bank statement, but whenever it doesn't inevitably I trace it to an arithmetic error by one of us rather than the bank's computer. (Once our bank's ATM ate a check I was trying to deposit without recording it on the screen or spewing a receipt, but a call to the bank found that despite the hardware glitch the money went into my account as intended.) Maybe some of you out there have stories to tell about goof-ups by banks and their computer systems, but my family's experience suggests automated banking errors are as rare as facial blemishes on Miss America.

However, if and when they do occur, I bet the reaction from customers would be even more blood curdling than in days of old when we waited in line to be serviced by bank tellers who occasionally miscounted the cash dispensed.

Our culture's Judeo-Christian ethic makes us forgiving of human fallibility. But we've become spoiled by the wondrous ways of modern technology, especially in critical applications concerning our lives and our money. So, we expect airplanes never to crash and the computers that manage our wealth and business transactions to operate flawlessly.

When a thankfully rare airline disaster does occur nowadays, it's more often traceable to human error rather than technical failure. Same with business blunders.

Murphy's Law

We've all heard of "Murphy's Law" – *anything that can go wrong will.* I don't know who that Murphy guy was who it's named after, but he was a keen observer of the human condition.

It's safe to say that everyone reading this has a tale or a hundred to tell of orders gone awry, quotations lost, wrong items shipped, deliveries to the wrong location, billing errors, returns not credited, and on and on. Almost always you can trace the ultimate cause to human error -- entering the wrong information, forgetting something, straying from standard procedure and so on. Software errors crop up from time to time, although that, too, is a result of human error by whoever programmed the computer.

What follows are some business tasks that in my experience are especially prone to mistakes.

- **Estimating**

It's been said only half in jest that when it comes to competitive bidding, if a contractor loses the job it means he bid too high, and if he lands the work, he must've bid too low. Labor estimating is filled with peril. Once you submit a quote to a customer, it's very difficult to come back later and say, "Oops, I forgot to include something. I hope you don't mind if I bump up the price we agreed upon."

114

Businesses that rely on bid markets often use computerized estimating programs, which factor in a bunch of variables that might arise. In construction contracting these include things like jobsite conditions and accessibility, weather, safety requirements, interaction with other trades and various other factors that can impact your labor or materials budget.

If you still use "scratch pad" estimating, good luck. At least have a checklist handy of variables likely to drive your costs up.

Veteran estimators who've submitted thousands of bids are inclined to think they know it all and don't need any prompts. I remind them that airline pilots with thousands of hours of flying time can pretty much do it all in their sleep, but the FAA still requires them to adhere to a checklist before taking off. That's a big reason why so few airplanes crash nowadays.

- **Ordering materials, merchandise & supplies**

Orders can go wrong in so many places. Estimated usage or the amount on hand could be off. Or, the person doing the ordering might transpose some of those tiny numbers in the catalog, or get the numbers right but the product turns out to be the wrong item for the application at hand. Or, all that information might be correct, but the person's handwriting can't be deciphered. Or, he sends it to someone whose printer is low on ink, making 8s look like 3s. Or, something said in a phone conversation gets garbled.

Or, you think you have certain things on hand and don't need to order them, but nobody really checks to make sure. So, when need arises you find out everything is available as you thought. It's a universal law that this always occurs at the same time as a snowstorm, machinery breakdown or one of a thousand other things that can occur to extend delivery lead times.

These things happen every day in every way. Mistakes made in material or equipment ordering are among the most painful, because they will follow the order at every step from beginning to end. And doesn't it always seem like mistake won't get noticed until someone is in desperate need of the items ordered.

- **Shipping and receiving**

By some miracle, the entire ordering process gets done accurately, but the guy picking the order in the supplier's warehouse is thinking about his Friday night date and picks the wrong part. Or, he loses track of the count and picks the wrong quantity.

Or, the guy in the shipping department doesn't notice the special instructions to deliver these items to a branch office and sends them to your central billing address instead. Nobody there knows what the heck this stuff is for, so they either tell the delivery person to take it back, or accept it but leave it to sit around the office until someone appears out of nowhere to identify it. Maybe they meant to ask the boss about it, but he's out and they went back to burying their heads in paperwork while the shipment sits in a corner, out of sight and mind. People in the branch office wonder where the heck is the stuff they ordered weeks ago and need now, but nobody thinks to ask anyone at headquarters, because why would it be there?

Oh, and while the guy in the warehouse was contemplating a steamy conclusion to his Friday night date, he inadvertently slapped Label A on Package B.

Just to add to the fun, the delivery driver didn't notice that this shipment calls for 11 boxes, but number 11 got bounced around and mixed with a different order, so he lost count and delivered only 10 boxes to your office.

Maybe none of this happened. Maybe the guys working in the warehouse and shipping dock did everything right. So, the right items in the right quantity with the right labels got sent to the right place. Except the driver got lost and spent hours trying to find your branch office. Your crew lost a day's worth of productivity as a result.

We live in a world surrounded by blunders galore.

- **Billing**

Errors in any of the previous categories almost always will lead to hectic times in the billing department. But sometimes the billing staff figures out creative ways to make mistakes of their own. They can invoice the wrong parts or the wrong quantity, or send the invoice to the wrong place. Back-ordered parts get charged twice or not at all. Or their invoices don't match the packing slips.

To err is no longer human

A big reason why businesses make so many mistakes is because they are so easy to shrug off. "Well, we've been really busy," is a common refrain. One can interpret that as saying a business is too busy making money to take care of business.

Other shrugs channel "to err is human" as if mistakes simply authenticate your humanity, which in a different context might be a badge of honor, I suppose. Problem is, your customers are far less inclined to shrug off your mistakes than you are. To them it doesn't make you more human, just less reliable.

Anyone running a business needs to get rid of the notion that mistakes will happen because we're all human. This may be literally true. Perfection may be unattainable in the real world. Yet unless you strive for 100% perfection you'll never come close enough to that ideal to run a successful business. Set your goal as 99% mistake-free transactions, and you're likely to run into trouble.

Would you buy a ticket on an airline whose planes made it to their destination 99% of the time? Would you continue to use bank ATMs if one out of a hundred times the machine miscounted your money?

The "nobody's perfect" mantra has become increasingly irrelevant in today's world. Competition and technology keep pushing the performance bar higher. People won't remember hundreds of transactions that took place without a hitch at your particular business. But they will remember every single one where you made a mistake. It's likely that was the one and only mistake you ever made with them, because odds are good they ditched you right afterward.

An accuracy rate of 99% means every day you may be leaving dozens of disgruntled customers trailing steam vapors as they gripe about your incompetence to everyone who will listen. You risk losing not only one unlucky customer, but the business of everyone s/he knows. Recall Customer Service Truth #2 from a previous chapter – on average, a dissatisfied customer tells *15 other people* about the problem. It doesn't take many mistakes for word to spread that your business is not to be trusted. Perfection may not be attainable in this life but people in business dare not breathe easily until that 99% satisfaction rate extends to a bunch of fractional decimals beyond.

The arithmetic of mistakes

Business mistakes are enormously costly when you examine all the hidden costs. Troubleshooting to find the cause of a mistake and then making good are activities almost certain to eat up whatever profit exists for a given transaction and then some.

NIBCO, a manufacturer of plumbing products and industrial valves, once undertook a process improvement program in which they discovered it took an average of *seven phone calls* by various individuals to correct a mistake in the ordering process. Think of your own experience trying to straighten out goof-ups in your everyday business or personal transactions. Making seven phone calls doesn't sound out of the ordinary, does it?

Think of how much human labor goes into seven phone conversations and following up with whatever actions are required. Figure out the pay scales of people involved in those conversations, the time it took them and what that computes to in dollars. Also factor in wasted opportunity cost. That is, time and effort unavailable for profitable activities.

Errors are a double-edged sword. They waste time and manpower fixing what's wrong, while at the same time taking those resources away from more productive activities aimed at generating sales and dazzling customers. Plus, they result in disappointed and angry customers who often must be mollified with discounts or other costly considerations. Can't you just sense a bunch of money swirling down a drain!

Mistakes are to profitability what a plane crash is to on-time arrival. Beyond all those phone calls, mistakes entail activity costs from returning, re-ordering, re-picking, re-packaging and re-shipping goods – often on an emergency basis. And/or, they result in service workers going back to redo work already done, using more materials, putting more mileage on vehicles and burning more gas in the process. While they are doing the profit-gobbling rework they are squandering opportunity dollars by being unavailable to service other customers who may be requesting profitable services.

What this does to your bottom line is rather stark. If your business operates with a 5% net profit margin, a $1,000 order nets you $50. Make a mistake with that order and you'll likely wipe out all of that profit and then some. Being conservative let's just assume that the mistake costs only $50 in labor, material and overhead costs. So that flawed $1,000 order covers your expenses but leaves you with no profit. What this means is that if the next $1,000 in sales goes without a hitch and earns a net $50 in profit, your profit percentage for those two sales just dropped in half, to 2.5%.

In the real world it's likely the mistake will end up costing more than $50. If a mistake with that $1,000 transaction costs your business $100, that would mean you need to book $2,000 more in sales (without a mistake) to make up the money lost on the botched transaction. Some mistakes are even more costly. The arithmetic is daunting.

A news item from some years ago caught my eye about a real-world example of how costly a simple mistake can be. A Bass Pro Shops store was to be built in a new shopping center in Harlingen, Texas, requiring space for 1,000 cars and financed by the city's Economic Development Corporation. In converting square footage to square yards, the standard unit of measurement for parking lot pavements, an engineer multiplied by 27 instead of nine, tripling the amount of space of the parking lot. Officials estimated the mistake cost the city $920,000 in extra materials, bonding, insurance and tax expense. The engineer's blunder also led to sizable opportunity cost from all that unneeded parking space that could have been put to better use.

In 2003 I wrote an article for Supply House Times magazine about electronic transactions in the electrical industry between manufacturers and distributors. It concerned a study by the Industry Data Exchange Association (IDEA), an e-commerce service provider.

IDEA examined almost 74,000 product code records submitted by 10 manufacturers and eight distributors participating in the study. The purpose was to find the degree to which manufacturer data matched distributor data. Some highlights of the findings:

- Only 5% of the records matched between the manufacturer and distributor on all fields.
- 21% of the records matched the manufacturer and the distributor product codes, but were blank or zero on one or more fields, i.e., part number, minimum quantity, price and units of measure.
- 40% of the records were found only in the manufacturer data files.
- 12% of the records were found only in the distributor data files.
- 60% of the total items were mismatched in critical order data and invoice fields.
- Some 30,000 items were in the manufacturers' systems, but not in the distributors' systems. These items were therefore not visible by the distributors and thus potentially a source of lost sales.
- More than 8,700 items were only in the distributors' systems. These would be a major source of transaction errors caused when distributors attempted to order products that didn't exist in the manufacturers' systems. This would lead to time-consuming manual intervention at either end on purchase orders and invoices.

Costs attributed to all these errors were estimated by IDEA to be about 1% of sales for manufacturers and about .75% for distributors. That would eat up about a third of all the profit dollars for the average distributor. The dollar losses ranged from $73,000 for a $10 million distributor to $1.46 million for a $200 million firm — and even more for the manufacturers.

Detailed Procedures Help Eliminate Mistakes

In most industries, franchises have a much higher success rate than independent companies. That's because franchises leave nothing to chance. Virtually all of their operations represent best practices that have been written into a series of procedures governing everything from how to keep the books to how to greet customers to how to perform technical tasks.

That's why a McDonald's burger tastes the same, looks the same and is packaged the same whether you buy it from one of their outlets in Seattle or Miami or anywhere in between. Most franchises make it a condition of ownership that you have to follow their procedures to the letter.

Oh, but your business is as different as night and day from McDonald's, right? Actually, it's not as different as you might think. Think of how many repetitive tasks take place in your business day after day. After a while you perform them without hardly thinking but they really can be broken down into step-by-step instructions that if followed to the letter can virtually eliminate the chance of any mistakes.

Al Levi is a business consultant (www.appleseedbusiness.com) and big believer in detailing as many standard procedures as possible to run a business. Before he got into consulting he spent many years running OSI, his family's fuel oil and heating service company on Long Island, where he practiced what he now preaches by developing meticulous procedures for hundreds of field and office tasks. The example shown below was written many years ago to instruct technicians how to perform a routine steam boiler inspection and service. Notice how nothing is left to chance, beginning with ringing the homeowner's bell and wiping feet before entering.

OSI's proper procedures for a boiler clean & check
(Preliminary)
1. Ring bell or knock on door.

2. Wipe your feet and say, "Good morning or afternoon, Mrs. Jones."
3. Try to use back, side or basement doors. **Avoid the front door.** (Bold face in original document.)
4. Put down red resin paper if in doubt at all.
5. **Don't** pull out any electrical plugs for freezers, washing machines, dryers, etc., **unless necessary** and **you must leave your truck keys as a reminder by the plug**.
6. Don't turn off any burner switches on the staircase.
7. Take low voltage wire off relay or jumper off relay and put into safety.
8. Open cleanout doors and let the boiler cool off.

(Work begins)

1. Replace the nozzles.
2. Steel wool electrodes and take out of the holder and look for cracks.
3. Check end cone and look down the blast tube.
4. Clean pump and replace gasket.
5. Replace oil filer and all gaskets.
6. Check oil flow on inside tank and clean oil line if necessary.
7. Clean and check the fan blades.
8. Oil motors and bearing assemblies (if any).
9. Clean or replace gauge glass and always replace the washers.
10. Vacuum and clean the boiler, flue pipe and chimney base. Look outside for a chimney cleanout door.
11. Install wires back on relay, raise aquastat to start burner.
12. Start up burner (prime) and take pump pressure, and if two-pipe buried oil tank, take a vacuum test.
13. Flush low water cutoff and/or feeder while the burner is running. Burner should go off. **If not call office immediately**.
14. Perform a complete CO_2 test.
15. Lower the aquastat and clean the boiler jacket.
16. Clean up around the boiler-burner any rags, speedi-dri, stick-tite, etc., and remove from house.
17. Keep cleanup tickets in pocket and get them signed.

18. **Check all fittings for oil leaks just before you leave.**

19. Write on your tickets the following information: type of oil burner, name of boiler, if the job has an oil-fired water heater, size and spray pattern of the nozzles.

20. **Don't knock the last serviceman.** (This item shows a lot of class. Al Levi told me it was common for service technicians in his company's market to bash the efforts of competitors, and he didn't want his people stooping so low. I'll have more to say about bad-mouthing competitors in Chapter 8.)

Carrying a binder filled with detailed procedures like this, a new employee can go out and be productive with minimal training in a short period of time. And, this employee will represent the company in a way the owners want it to be represented.

Try to think of certain tasks your company performs over and over that could be detailed in the same way. Think of field operations, the way you handle phone calls and process paperwork, and so on. How many times has your business lost track of customer inquiries or complaints, or misplaced tools or materials, sent out wrong invoices or purchase orders, etc.? These things happen because somebody did something wrong. Maybe they forgot or neglected to follow instructions, or maybe were never taught precisely how to follow through on something.

Often the mistakes become institutionalized. That's because whoever taught a newcomer to do something may have inadvertently left something out. Think of how many times you've told an employee, "Oh, I forgot to tell you about ..." The new employee skips that step, and after a while that new employee becomes a veteran who trains a newcomer. Then it becomes a case of the blind leading the blind. Maybe the task still gets accomplished, but in a roundabout way that detracts from efficiency.

One of the advantages of a franchise or any business with multiple locations is that they can analyze which of their outlets has the best way of doing something and adapt that "best practice" to all of their facilities. Best practices also can be obtained from different employees in a single location. Maybe one person has a personal method of performing a task that works better than another person's way. You'll want everyone to adopt the best method, and the way to do that is to break it down step by step so you don't have to teach it over and over and maybe miss a step.

Most repetitive tasks can be broken down into 10 or 20 steps. Of course, every business entails hundreds of repetitive tasks, so it is rather laborious and time consuming to break each once down – but only the first time. Once the steps are written down the guidance can last almost forever, with occasional revisions to accommodate new technology or better methodology.

If you make it a goal to produce one or two of these task descriptions every day, within a year or less you could have every relevant task covered, and your business would reap the benefits forever. These lasting benefits include:

- Speeds up training and productivity of new employees.
- Make sure everyone does things the way you want them done.
- Helps eliminate mistakes.
- When mistakes do get made, written procedures help to track down their causes by analyzing which steps were skipped or done wrong. This enables you to correct mistakes and hold people accountable.
- Lowers your costs due to greater efficiency and fewer mistakes.
- Enables owners and managers to identify bottlenecks and problem areas.
- Instills a sense of teamwork among the staff, who are all working the same way toward common goals.
- Frees up productive time for owners and managers who don't have to explain things in detail over and over.
- Most important, you are likely to have more satisfied customers, because not nearly as many things will go wrong with your services.

One other benefit may not come into play for a long time but could turn out to be huge. Systematizing your business enhances its marketability if you ever want to sell it.

When it comes time to retire or do something else, many small business owners find out that nobody wants to buy their business or only at a lowball price. That's because many small businesses have nothing substantial to sell except the owner's moxie and customer relationships. Once the owner leaves, there's not much worthwhile acquiring.

Think of a successful restaurant whose owner happens to be a fabulous chef. If that owner keeps all the recipes in his/her head and decides to leave, that business is worth not much more than the value of its tables, chairs and silverware. But if all the recipes are documented to the last pinch of salt, anyone can come in to recreate the cuisine that makes the restaurant successful.

Many small business owners take an almost perverse pride in operating unsystematically. They prefer to let their gut instincts guide them and maybe deep down inside get a kick out of being indispensable. But if you ever want to sell a business you own, you are much better off doing everything you can to detail its procedures to the point where it can operate without you.

Measure Twice, Cut Once

That old carpenter's adage holds another key to eliminating mistakes in business. It takes very little extra time to measure twice. However, it's very costly in material and labor to cut something to the wrong length and have to do it all over again.

The "measure twice" mentality can be applied to all business activities, especially when it comes to paperwork. Inaccurate paperwork is a leading cause of mistakes. Many mistakes can be avoided with simple common-sense practices such as repeating verbal orders back to customers, double-checking all paperwork and training everyone in the order processing chain on proper procedures – better yet, creating written step-by-step procedures as just discussed.

When discussing an order or quote with customers, get in the habit of repeating all of the product descriptions, quantities and prices. Make sure the customer verifies all the information before concluding the transaction. Ask the customer if s/he's sure about sizes, colors and other variables that in your experience might have caused trouble in the past. Then double-check all of the information on your paperwork before submitting it. Make sure your handwriting is legible. Finally, make sure it gets routed correctly.

All of these steps become routine after a while. Yet that's precisely the reason mistakes are so common. People perform certain procedures so often it's easy to become careless. As workloads increase, you go faster and faster. You try to multi-task and perform too many functions at once -- such as processing the paperwork from one customer while speaking to another on the phone. The busier you get, the more tempting it is to take such shortcuts.

And the more shortcuts you take, the more mistakes you are likely to make.

Concentrate on the task at hand. With experience you will become more productive by doing things faster, but it's never a good tradeoff to sacrifice accuracy for speed. If you don't provide accurate information to the warehouse, the order will not be pulled or shipped correctly. If you don't provide accurate information to accounts receivable, billing will be wrong. If you don't adjust inventory, future purchasing will be off.

"Measure twice" also applies to the work of others. You have control over your own activities. Unfortunately, the mistakes that bite you often are caused by other participants in a supply chain, both inside and outside of your company.

Never assume that documents originated or approved by others must be accurate. Double-check to make sure your company has in stock what you've committed to deliver. Go the extra mile for customers – and for yourself, because mistakes cost you plenty of money. Even worse, mistakes result in unhappy customers who are unlikely to continue patronizing your business.

Ounces of prevention

Another slogan worth embracing is "an ounce of prevention is worth a pound of cure." Avoiding mistakes is a lot less costly than correcting them.

Easier said than done, of course. So many things can go wrong the wonder is not that mistakes get made, but that anything in the business world ever gets done right! Here are some practices and things to keep in mind to help cut down the simple mistakes that occur time and time again in businesses large and small.

1. Repetition.

Many business communications are verbal. You refer to products by name and number, you call for additions or adjustments, and you quote selling prices over the phone. That's a lot of information when you think about it. Even routine transactions have a lot of opportunities for misinformation to be transmitted or received.

That's why it's important to concentrate on speaking clearly. Check and double-check code numbers. Ask the recipient of the information to read back what s/he took down.

When discussing an order or quote, get in the habit of repeating all of the order numbers, product descriptions, quantities and prices. Then double-check all of the information you have entered in your computer or on your paperwork before submitting it. If you are hand-writing an order, make sure your handwriting is legible.

2. Take a cue from the military.

Military communications often involve matters of life and death. It's easy to confuse certain sounds – especially when there's gunfire in the background -- and that's why the military has established word counterparts for each letter of the alphabet, i.e., Alpha (A), Bravo (B), Charlie (C), etc. It's a good idea to get in the habit of using military-like word counterparts when reciting product descriptions and part numbers. For instance: "I need to know how many items we have in stock of product number FTS1234. That's Foxtrot, Tango, Sam, one, two three, four."

Doing all this takes a little longer, but nothing slows you down more than correcting mistakes. It pays to take time to speak slowly and enunciate clearly when reciting order information, and to ask the recipient to repeat the information back to you.

3. "Smell" test.

Do things "smell" right to you? Does it make sense to suddenly see an order for 10 items normally ordered one at a time? Is that piece of equipment different than anything this customer has ever ordered before?

4. Verification.

Don't assume that just because you've checked and double-checked everything on your end, the information will get transmitted and absorbed accurately. Repeat verbally things you see on paperwork and ask the other party to verify that all the information is correct. Where appropriate, ask them to acknowledge receipt of important messages. E-mail makes this easy to do by simply hitting the reply button.

5. Red-flag alert.

One aspect of the verification process that always raises a red flag with me is when the other party says, "I think that's right ... I'm pretty sure about that ... As far as I know ...." My response always is, "Do you think that's right, or do you KNOW it's right?" – putting the onus on them to double-check. I've nipped quite a few errors in the bud using this tactic.

6. Send to the right person and place.

When I was employed as a magazine editor hardly a week would go by without mail coming to me via our corporate headquarters that was 300 miles away. My business address was available for anyone to see on our magazine's masthead and website but in the real-world databases seldom get updated. Also keep in mind that delivery and billing addresses frequently are different. If you can target delivery to a specific person rather than just a company, it increases the chance of it landing in the right place. The internet makes it simple to verify information.

7. Accountability.

Hold people responsible for avoiding mistakes. Document whenever it happens and make it a part of their performance review. Better yet, set up a bonus program for mistake-free performance. Positive incentives generally get better results than punishments.

Chapter 7 – The Biggest Mistakes Of All

Small Businesses Are Easy To Fleece

Industrial Valco (IV), a Southern California-based distributor of industrial valves and fittings, is a successful family business staffed with many long-term employees. Trust comes naturally within a group of people used to working around family and longtime friends. That's why it took them so long to realize that a controller they had hired in the mid-2000s was ripping them off to the tune of $830,000 over a five-year period.

According to IV President Rob Raban, "He was a hard worker and people liked him." His performance seemed good for a long time, but eventually he got fired when Raban became exasperated over continual problems getting timely financial reports — "All we heard was computer problems and other excuses." After terminating the man, IV contracted with a financial expert to sort things out, and within a couple of days discovered a phony payroll scheme

I asked Raban what he learned from the experience and what to do differently. Here are key points:

- "I did a background check before hiring the guy, but not as deep as I should have." References were checked, which were all complimentary, but it's easy for a crook to recruit friends or relatives to masquerade as former employers. It could also be that he was straight with his former employers or cheated but was not discovered. "One thing I didn't check was his graduation certificate," said Raban. The man claimed to have a certain college degree but didn't. Lesson: "You need to contact the college directly and have them send you the certificate and transcript."

- The man was an extremely hard worker who frequently stayed late and never took days off or vacations. This is one of the classic warning signs of an embezzler. They fear that during time away someone might probe the books and discover them.
- Another obvious warning sign is inordinate wealth in relation to pay scale. IV's former controller drove an expensive car, though Raban said he had covered those tracks by claiming to be from a wealthy family.
- Lesson learned, Raban worked with a labor attorney to develop questions to ask, and hired a financial consultant to interview new controller candidates. "That's important, bringing in an expert for the interview process," he stressed. "I know industrial valves and don't need to hire an outsider when it comes to warehouse or sales positions. But I don't know CFO stuff." The financial expert was expensive but ultimately cost far less than the pilfered $830,000, and IV's replacement controller worked out fine.
- "My biggest mistake was just giving him too much power," said Raban of the embezzler. "He had a background in computers and we were transitioning computer systems, so he was given a lot of authority with both the computer setup and on the financial side."

IV's former controller ended up with a prison sentence and was forced to make restitution, although IV was never able to collect the full amount he stole from the business. Unfortunately, this was one of many stories I'd written over the years about small businesses getting ripped off by people entrusted with company finances and bookkeeping.

An even bigger ripoff victimized a large mechanical contractor in the Phoenix area who estimated losses at $1.9 million over an eight-year period by a bookkeeper with a gambling problem. On another occasion I reported on a plumbing contractor who told me of attending the lavish wedding of a key employee's daughter and wondering how the man could afford the extravagance. After investigating he learned the wedding was unwittingly financed by his own business coffers.

Another plumbing contractor told me of losing about $40,000 to a bookkeeper with a gambling problem – an amount that could have been much larger, except this company actually had controls in place to guard against embezzlement. During my career I also got wind of several trade associations whose staff executives had gotten away with hanky-panky due to lack of sufficient oversight from the volunteer board members.

Costly paperwork crimes

Employee theft is a major problem for many businesses that keep large inventories of goods and/or deal in cash. Most vulnerable business owners are mindful of this and take reasonable security precautions to guard against warehouse workers and truck drivers sneaking off with $20 gadgets under their coats. Yet most have blinders on when it comes to far costlier theft by white collar staffers who know how to manipulate paperwork.

It's hard to keep track of all the schemes thought up by clever inside crooks. Payments get made to phony companies for goods and services not rendered. Payroll clerks boost earnings via jacked-up paychecks, bonuses or expense reimbursements. Legitimate checks end up in the wrong bank accounts via forgery. Companies overpay for inferior goods thanks to vendor kickbacks. A receiving clerk logs 9 items when he received 10. A receivables clerk makes money owed vanish from the records. A checkout clerk holds a finger over the bar code when swiping to fool the security camera.

Tax payments get skipped because the money has been siphoned away. This one is a BIG DEAL and a fairly common scam by crooked bookkeepers and financial officers charged with paying taxes. Many owners discover hanky-panky when notified by the IRS that they owe back payments. The government may express condolences, but they'll still want their money.

I'm not smart enough and maybe a bit too honest to know all the ways white collar theft can suck the lifeblood out of your business. But plenty of clever crooks are out there thinking up new schemes or, more often, falling back on tried and true methods of relieving businesses of their legitimate profits.

I continue to be astonished by how many small businesses fall victim to fraud and embezzlement by trusted employees. According to a 2010 study by the Association of Certified Fraud Examiners, organizations worldwide lose an estimated 5% of their annual revenues to fraud, potentially reaching more than $2.9 trillion. They examined 1,843 companies around the world, 60% of which were from the U.S., and uncovered a median loss of $160,000. About 25% of the cases examined involved a loss of $1 million or more. The American Management Association attributes around 20% of all business failures as the direct result of employee theft.

Google "small business embezzlement," and you'll find an array of news stories of recent vintage. One told of a realty office manager in Nevada sent to prison for 10 years after being convicted of stealing almost $500,000 from the business over a four-year period via fraudulent checks, doctored accounting logs and payments to bogus accounts. That was the amount the thief admitted to, though investigators believe her total pilferage topped $1 million. Her schemes unraveled when the IRS told the business owner – who until then considered the office manager her best friend -- that she owed more than $550,000 in payroll withholding taxes, a task that was the office manager's duty to pay. The convicted office manager got word of her bust while on a cruise sponsored by a local casino, of which see was a top customer. Gambling debts are a frequent story line in many embezzlement cases.

The stories go on and on. It takes a mastermind to get away with embezzling from a Fortune 500 firm because large companies employ an army of accountants and auditors, and they have checks and balances that make it hard for any single individual to get away with much.

Small businesses and trade organizations are much easier pickings. Embezzlers seek out small organizations precisely because so many of their proprietors tend to be inattentive to bookkeeping and are happy to hand over those duties. Small organizations often have only one or two people apart from the owner with access to all the payments and collections records.

If an owner has no background in accounting and finance the temptation is great to hire an experienced controller or CFO who may be the only one who truly understands a firm's financial accounting system.

Small-business embezzlers don't even need to be very sophisticated, just a little perceptive in noticing that owners and key managers choose to see and hear no evil. Embezzlers often have engaging personalities and ingratiate themselves into positions of trust with small business employers. Many small business owners come to regard employees like family and find it hard to fathom any engaged in wrongdoing.

Red flags

Not every embezzler joins a company with larceny in mind. Some start out as honest employees and may work for years without stealing a dime. This builds trust and it's why in so many cases a shocked employer finds "the last person I would suspect" pilfered megabucks from the company.

Over time the embezzler may be driven by a gambling problem or economic hardship to seek additional income. At the start they may even intend to pay it back after they "get back on their feet." Those good intentions are almost never followed through.

Typically, embezzlers start out stealing small amounts. Once they find they can get away with it they steadily up the ante. A lot of them could get away with it indefinitely if they stuck to stealing sums that are inconsequential to the business. Almost all succumb to greed in the long run, however.

Sometimes money is not even the main motive. Many embezzlers turn out to be disgruntled employees who believe they are underpaid and underappreciated. To their way of thinking, they are simply ironing out an unfair disparity between their worth and their compensation.

Like IV's larcenous controller described at the start of this chapter, many embezzlers put in long hours and seem to be the hardest workers in a company. Often they decline to take sick days and vacation time off. Although not every workaholic is a crook, extreme dedication to the job is one of the top red flag alerts for potential embezzlement.

Gambling problems top the list of red flags. Keep your radar tuned to employees who spend a lot of time in casinos or an inordinate amount of time organizing betting pools, card games and so on. Make it a terminable offense if anyone uses your organization's computers to visit sports books and online gaming sites.

Other red flags:

- An employee seeming to live beyond his/her means. Sometimes there's an innocent explanation, like a high-income spouse or an inheritance, but keep your guard up.
- A drinking problem. Alcoholism doesn't necessarily go hand-in-hand with thievery, but alcoholics tend toward a variety of deviant behavior and may be driven in part by money problems.
- Association with people of questionable character.
- A key employee who refuses to accept a promotion or change jobs.
- An inexplicable drop in profits.
- Excessive inventory shrinkage.
- Sloppy recordkeeping and/or unexplained changes in your recordkeeping system.
- Unreasonable explanations to questions about finances.
- Unfamiliar customers with numerous purchases or credits.
- Mysterious vendors.
- Delayed bank deposits or excessive account discrepancies.
- Customers complaining about being billed for money already paid.
- A surge in past due accounts receivable.
- Duplicate payments.
- Close personal friendship with a customer or supplier. (This is a good thing in most cases, but keep your eyes peeled for potential collusion that costs you money.)

Trust, But Verify

Complacency is an easy trap to fall into as a small business owner. Many of your employees may have been with you a long time and are like family. You regard them as good, honest people and you've never seen any reason not to trust them.

Your instincts are probably correct. I've written about thousands of small, closely-held businesses over the years and the vast majority of them employ trustworthy people. The last thing I want to do is instigate unwarranted suspicion.

Nonetheless ...

Reasonable precautions need not intrude upon the quality of your employee relationships. It's okay to trust the people who work for you, but if they are trustworthy they should have no qualms if you put systems in place to verify that trust. Here are some simple steps that may prevent big losses.

- **Review bank statements**

Corporate bank statements should be mailed directly to the owner's home. Review them each month and make a list of any checks made out to vendors whose names you do not recognize or for amounts that seem too high. Look for signature forgeries.

Yes, these statements may run quite a few pages, but you're not looking to analyze every transaction, just a handful that seem aberrant. This is a wise practice even without the embezzlement issue. It will help you get a handle on unnecessary or excessive expenditures.

- **Require double signatures on all organization checks**

Ideally, one of them ought to be an owner's, but if you fear writer's cramp at least require the signature of two top managers. Fraud could still occur if they collude, but that's a lot less likely than with any single individual having check-writing authority.

Small businesses that write a lot of checks each month sometimes require double signatures only on amounts above a certain level. This can work okay but then keep your eyes peeled for an excessive number of small payments.

- **Divide responsibilities**

Don't put the same person in charge of payables and receivables; of purchasing and inventory control; of sales and shipping. Above all, never give a single person apart from the owner authority to write checks, make deposits and balance the monthly bank statement.

Dividing responsibilities is easier said than done in tiny companies with only a handful of employees. Multitasking is inevitable for some mom and pop businesses. In those cases one of the owners should at least try to maintain control of the key activities noted in the previous paragraph.

- **Require employees to take earned vacation days**

Mental health considerations alone make this a wise policy. Be suspicious of anyone who declines to take time off no matter how sick and who puts in unusually long hours.

- **Pay attention to the P & L**

Every business owner should produce and meticulously review a "Profit & Loss" statement at least monthly, and weekly or even daily is advisable. The "P & L" is a financial snapshot of your business at that point in time, breaking down sources of income versus itemized expenditures. It is an indispensable business management tool, and also can serve as a fraud detector by revealing financial irregularities.

Some slumps may be attributable to market forces. Other times a P & L will reveal operational shortcomings. If you probe deeply enough you may find out that analysis of margins, turnover rates, cost of goods sold, past due receivables and other metrics can unravel fraud or embezzlement as well.

- **Hire an outside auditor**

Annual reconciling of financial records should be an automatic part of your business cycle. But don't put inmates in charge of the asylum. Have a reputable, independent CPA firm evaluate your accounting systems and practices – and don't automatically hire one recommended by your controller/CFO.

- **Do civil as well as criminal background checks**

Embezzlers who get caught don't always end up in criminal court. Sometimes a business may choose to avoid the expense and bad publicity of filing criminal charges and simply sue an embezzler in a civil court to retrieve the funds. Some embezzlers get fired and hired time after time because they never get convicted of the crime. Contact the Association of Certified Fraud Examiners to inquire about civil background checks. www.acfe.com.

- **Consider fidelity bond insurance**

If you feel your business is particularly vulnerable to fraud, ask your insurer about fidelity insurance for employees who handle your finances. This is a form of insurance that comes with various particulars but in general covers a business for losses incurred by dishonest acts. Besides covering losses, another benefit is that the insurer will do thorough background checks on all employees named in the policy.

- **Physical inventory counts**

An annual physical inventory count is standard practice for retailers and wholesalers who buy and sell a lot of merchandise. It's a painstaking process ("a pain in the anatomy" is how most describe it) for companies that sell thousands of items, but the only way to truly reconcile the amount of goods on hand with what the computer tells you is available.

A certain amount of discrepancy with inventory records can be expected because people do make honest mistakes. But if you operate a large store or warehouse filled with valuable merchandise, you can go broke before knowing it if the shrinkage gets out of hand.

Strangers At The Door

Nobody saw it coming. The guy apparently didn't have a record and had passed a criminal background check before being hired as an installer by a cable company in my hometown of Chicago. I say "apparently" because there is no national database on criminal records, and bad guys can sneak through the hodge-podge of documentation.

So, the creep was arrested and charged with the sexual assault and murder of a young woman who let him into her home to repair her internet service. He was a suspect in the murder of another woman two months before under similar circumstances. The cops didn't tell his employer he was a suspect because there wasn't enough evidence to arrest him. (He subsequently was charged with the first murder as well.)

Stuff like this doesn't happen every day, but there's always a chance of it happening when people open their door to strangers going about legitimate business. And while home service technicians don't commit lurid murders every day, every day does bring a slew of lesser crimes by workers voluntarily let into homes and offices.

Residential service contractors dread getting complaints about things missing from the home after a visit from one of their service techs, and many of them have had the experience at one time or another. Clever thieves can last a long time on a payroll because they know how to disguise their crimes. Missing jewelry might not get noticed for days or even weeks after a service call. Sometimes the theft doesn't occur during the visit, but in a subsequent break-in.

I recall another local story about a computer repair technician whose job took him to various office sites. Women who worked in those offices often reported purses and other personal belongings missing. The thief got busted when investigators put two and two together and noticed the correlation between his service calls and the office thefts.

Those of you who run businesses involving visits to homes or commercial work sites have an obligation to make sure you hire people of impeccable personal character. One unsavory worker on the payroll can destroy your company.

You need to work hard at it. Criminal background checks are no guarantee you'll discover the deepest, darkest secrets of job applicants. But it's virtually guaranteed that you won't discover them – until it's too late – without doing background checks.

Chapter 8 – Simple Mistakes, Easy Solutions

Turn Bad Practices Into Best Ones

I once interviewed a kitchen and bath dealer in Florida for a magazine article. Upon pulling into his parking lot I noticed a Home Depot right across the street. The facility included an "Expo Store," which until Home Depot pulled the plug on the concept in 2009 was Big Orange's attempt to muscle in on the luxury kitchen-bath remodeling business. Wow, I remarked to the independent dealer, that must be tough to compete against!

Actually, he told me he was thrilled when Home Depot opened up across the road. That's because he knew he would get spillover business from customers who couldn't find what they were looking for or weren't satisfied with the offerings there. This dealer made it a point to get to know Home Depot's store manager, who often referred customers to him for goods and services not offered by the big box store. This wise store manager understood that it was in his best interest to have customers walk out the door feeling well served, even if they didn't make any purchases that day. Doing so made it likely they would return, as well as say positive things about Home Depot to friends and neighbors.

The lesson here is that old saw about problems being opportunities in disguise. It's common for small business owners to look at competitors as enemies, but if you look hard enough you just might find ways to get to win-win with them.

This leads off a compilation of common business mistakes that are not killers by themselves, but when accumulated they can mark a business as ripe for failure.

Respect your competition

Hating the competition is a natural instinct for many small business owners. After all, those are the people taking bread off your table.

Stinkin' thinkin'. Bad-mouthing competitors has a way of soiling your own reputation. Most people don't like hearing trash talk, especially if they sometimes patronize and perhaps like the business getting trashed. For all you know, the customer you're talking to could be related to the competitor.

Besides, if competitors are taking business away from you, maybe you can learn something from them. Instead of treating them like enemies, try to get to know them. Join them in Chamber of Commerce activities and seek to befriend them. You just might learn whatever it is they're doing right that you're not.

A few days before writing this I tried out a new restaurant that recently opened down the street from my residence. I chatted with the owner who began bragging about how much better his food was than that of various local competitors and singled out several for derision. One of them is a neighborhood bar/restaurant that happens to be one of my favorite hangouts, whose delicious home-made meals usually fill my belly about once a week. They will continue to get my business. Guess who won't.

Embrace your community

This is a no-brainer. Most small businesses draw considerable patronage from their immediate neighborhood, and even if you sell to far-flung markets, it's beneficial to be recognized as an upstanding local citizen. So, join the Chamber of Commerce, Better Business Bureau, Rotary and Optimist Clubs, etc. Throw some ad dollars at local sports terms and church bulletins, donate your goods or services to local charity drives. Becoming a part of these organizations and activities conveys instant credibility for a new business.

I've never heard of any small business spending themselves into bankruptcy supporting local institutions. I suspect many have been saved from bankruptcy by patronage generated through such efforts.

Embrace the internet and social media

Depending on your type of business, a website may or may not be crucial to your marketing efforts. Yet almost everyone visits business websites these days to obtain basic information and you don't want to be perceived as not "with it."

Hire a capable website designer. Tell that person you want a website that conveys credibility and is easy to use with simple site navigation. For most small businesses, no information should be more than three menu clicks away. Be sure your phone number and email address are prominently displayed and easily accessible as soon as a visitor enters your site. If applicable, enable online credit card payment for immediate sales.

Facebook and Twitter are increasingly used by businesses as marketing tools. This writer confesses to being behind the curve with their use, but I know enough to know that I don't know enough about social media. And, I sense that this is the modern version of "word of mouth," and immensely more powerful than ever. Find someone who does get it, and ask them to help you get with it.

Network rather than hang out

Most businesspeople understand the value of "networking." What most don't understand is how to do it effectively. Networking is more than rubbing elbows and chit-chatting over cocktails. That's not networking, that's hanging out. While it may make for an enjoyable evening, it doesn't usually result in productive business leads unless you couple it with some other tactics as follows.

- **Hang out with people you don't know.**

Most people who attend business social functions spend most of their time mingling with friends and co-workers. They form a tight conversational circle and dine at the same table – even tipping chairs forward to save spots for their buddies.

You can hang out with friends at any time and place. When an opportunity presents itself for business networking, force yourself to stray from your "tribe" and introduce yourself to people you don't know. Make it a point to sit at a luncheon or dinner table populated by some strangers.

- **Seek out movers and shakers.**

The average person has a sphere of influence of about 50 people. That is about the number of friends and family members apt to follow their recommendations. However, the "movers and shakers" in any given community have spheres of influence that number in the hundreds or even thousands. Seek out these persons in the crowd, make conversation and get to know them. Join the same community and social organizations they do. Do volunteer work for charities they are associated with.

- **Treat everyone with respect.**

Some people in the group may wield very little business influence, and you don't want to waste the entire evening talking to them. But avoid being abrupt and impolite in breaking off conversations.

At one level this is simply a matter of common courtesy, but it also entails considerable business logic. That lowly bank teller may be the son-in-law of the bank president and in a few years may be the head of commercial lending. Be especially deferential to people who work as secretaries or administrative assistants to important people. They are "gatekeepers" who control access to the boss. Befriending them can be even more productive than going straight for the big shot who may brush you off. Try to leave everyone with a good impression of you.

- **Talk about their interests, not your own.**

The one subject a VIP will always find fascinating is himself/herself. Ask open-ended and feel-good questions as conversation starters, such as:

How long have you been in business?
How did you get started?
What do you enjoy most about your work?

What are the biggest problems you face in business?
Who are your best customers?

Notice the one common denominator in these sample conversation starters – the word *you* or *your*. If you talk enough about the other party, sooner or later that person is apt to start inquiring about you and your business. But avoid talking about yourself until then. Keep the conversation focused on them. Perverse as it may seem, this is the way to get them to think of you as an interesting person!

If they do ask about your business, keep it brief. Cocktail conversations are not the place to narrate your entire business history. That's when VIPs' eyes glaze over and they start looking over your shoulder for other people to make conversation with.

Be prepared with what's known as an "elevator speech." This is a concise statement of who you are and what you do that can be delivered in about 20 seconds – the amount of time it takes for an elevator to go between floors. The objective is to make a first impression on the person of influence. If you do this well, it can lead to more substantive business meetings down the road where you can fill in the details.

- **Collect business cards.**

It's more important to collect business cards than to pass yours out. The exchange of business cards is a ritual that usually concludes with most cards getting tossed in a wastebasket or junk drawer. You can't control what the other party does with yours. But once you obtain a card from a mover and shaker, you have it in your power to follow up with further contacts.

- **Position yourself by the entrance.**

In large gatherings it's easy to miss people you want to see. The best way to ensure contact with people you are anxious to meet is to hang out near the main entrance, and stay there. VIPs may not make it to every corner of a room, but they all must pass through the entryway.

- **Be prepared.**

Have your business cards in a convenient pocket so you don't have to be fumbling around for them. Bring along a small notebook and pen to jot down notes of important things people say to you.

If the information is the least bit sensitive, wait until the person moves along before taking out your notebook. In some situations, however, it can be advantageous to take notes right in front of the person. This conveys the impression that you are paying attention and regard what they say as important. You'll need to use judgment and play this one by ear.

Proofread, proofread, proofread

Whenever I see a typographical error in promotional literature, it tends to slam the door on that business for me. Maybe this stems from professional neurosis, but I think most literate people have misgivings when they see sloppiness show up in any business activity. Nobody wants to eat in a restaurant with dirty tables, and by the same token many of us don't want to patronize any business whose inattentiveness to detail is on display for all to see.

I once saw a plumber's truck drive by on which the owner's occupation was spelled "plummer." He may know everything there is to know about fixing leaks but he'll never get a chance to prove it to me.

Maybe you weren't an A student in English. But plenty of people with degrees in English are out of work, and you can hire them as proofreaders at bargain rates.

Accept all coupons

Have you ever suffered the indignity of presenting a discount coupon to some business and having it refused for being out of date? Didn't your regard for that business drop through the floor?

Such a silly mistake. What's the point of issuing discount coupons? It's to attract prospective customers who you hope will return many times over paying full price. So what sense does it make to turn them away because of an arbitrary deadline?

Actually, putting deadlines on coupons does make sense. It helps you measure returns from coupon runs, and instills a sense of urgency in customers to visit you soon. But don't turn a coupon that's supposed to be a business driver into a barrier. Accept them even if late. Better still, inform the customer that the coupon is outdated, but you'll accept it anyway as a goodwill gesture.

If your business utilizes discount coupons, go it even one better. Accept competitors' coupons – and advertise that fact. ("We accept all coupons!") The coupons will still do what they're intended to do – draw prospective customers -- except you'll be the beneficiary while a competitor pays the printing bill.

Guarantee satisfaction

Many small businesses make it an ordeal for customers to return merchandise or obtain refunds for goods and services they are not satisfied with. This is short-sighted. Yes, it will cost a little money upfront to retract a sale, but failing to make amends will likely lose that customer forever and cause him/her to depart with ill will toward your business.

Notice how many successful businesses use "100% Satisfaction Guaranteed" in their advertising and promotional messages. It is a way to build trust and buy goodwill that will be paid back many times during the life of your business. Stop thinking in terms of single transactions. Aim to recruit customers for life.

Spread yourself out

Some businesses thrive right from the start thanks to a single great customer that provides a large percentage of revenues. That's dangerous. Try to diversify your customer base as much as possible.

Know your limits

Ambition is a wonderful trait but beware of blind ambition in tackling projects over your head. The dollar volume seems irresistible but maybe the project, the financing or the manpower requirements are far beyond what you've ever handled before. Maybe the customer is someone you've never worked with before and maybe there's a bad reputation lingering in the background. The schedule might strike you as unrealistic, but heck, you'll just push a little harder.

It can be a fine line between growing your business to the next level and biting off more than you can chew. Envision a worst-case scenario, then ask yourself, are you betting the company? Can you survive if this particular project crashes?

Avoid bidding wars

For businesses that rely on competitive bidding for work, pay attention to the number of bidders. When bids are in abundance, the job usually goes to the one who makes the biggest mistake. I once read of a study showing that when there are as many as a dozen bidders on a construction contract, the "winning" bidder almost always loses money on the project. Before you go out and celebrate winning a job from among a large crowd of bidders, better crunch those numbers every which way to see if you can identify where you made a mistake.

Sell UP before selling down

A fundamental principle of salesmanship is to "sell up by selling down." That is, get in the habit of pitching your best, most expensive products and services first, and then working your way down if customers flinch at the higher price tags.

Most small businesspeople go in the opposite direction. They start by showing the cheapest offerings first and then try to entice customers to move up in quality and price. That doesn't work as well as starting at the top of the line because you may do too good a job selling the lower end. If a customer perceives that a cheaper offering satisfies his/her needs, s/he will stop there and resist paying more even if the quality is better. By starting at the top, you draw attention to features and benefits the customer may find appealing and be unwilling to give up at a lower price.

Sell features rather than benefits

This is probably the most common mistake made by inexperienced sellers. Features are the visible or measurable qualities of a product or service. Benefits are what those features can do for the buyer. For instance, a 95% efficiency rating for a furnace is a feature of that product. The benefit is substantial fuel savings. Four-wheel drive is an attractive feature in a vehicle, but only because it results in the benefit of greater traction that enables better handling on dirt roads, steep hills and icy surfaces.

Dan Holohan (www.heatinghelp.com), who I introduced in Chapter 4, used the following example in his *Just Add H2Oh!* Book to illustrate the difference between features and benefits. He first drew attention to a boiler company's advertisement containing this information:

- 92% AFUE
- Direct Vent
- Sealed Combustion
- Compact Cabinet
- Low NOX
- Low Mass
- Low Temp.
- Shock Proof
- No Minimum Water Temperature

"Now, you're a home owner. Did you get any of this?" Dan asked. So much for the features of that boiler being advertised.

Here's how Dan proposed to present that same information in terms of benefits deriving from those features:

- "Chimneys take up valuable living space, so we did away with them!"
- "Our boiler is so small you won't even know it's there."
- "With our boiler, you'll get more comfort for every dollar you spend on fuel. Try as you might, you won't find a boiler that costs less to operate from year to year."
- "Our boiler doesn't pollute the air you and your children breathe."

- "We designed our boiler specifically for modern radiant heating systems."

Much better, wouldn't you agree?

Advertise for results

Some types of businesses live or die by advertising, while for others it is unimportant. For the most part, though, advertising works. We wouldn't be exposed to thousands of advertising messages each day if it didn't.

An old adage in the advertising field is that half of all ad dollars are wasted. It's just that nobody can identify which half.

There's a lot of truth to that saying. Advertising can be divided into two categories:

1. Institutional advertising attempts to build name and brand identity. It doesn't lend itself to identifiable gains to business, though most advertising pros recommend spending at least a portion of your advertising budget on institutional ads. Examples include billboards, print media, even the signage on company vehicles.

2. Direct response advertising is measurable, and where the lion's share of most small business advertising ought to be directed. Direct response ads include telephone directories, discount coupons and, especially, electronic media where you can measure the number and types of inquiries received.

The most common mistake made by small businesses when it comes to advertising is not sustaining it. Ad sales reps often hear statements like, "I'll buy an ad to see if it works. If it does, I'll buy some more."

When it comes to advertising exposure, once is not enough. It does little good to buy a single ad in a newspaper, magazine, or any other medium, or to send out a single mailing to prospective customers. The chances that a prospect will just happen to see your ad the one time you just happen to advertise are very slim.

Big ads generally work better than small ads. However, if you have a limited budget most advertising pros will tell you that you can get better bang for your buck running smaller ads frequently rather than larger ads once in a while. Size is not as much a factor in advertising success as repetition.

There are a many reasons why you must repeat advertising for it to be effective. Michael Gerber, author of the renowned *Guerilla Marketing* series of business books, identified 10 of them.

1.People are busy.

The first time they see your ad, they may be interested in your services but have other commitments that take precedence. If they saw your ad a second time, or third time, they might take action.

2. They forget it.

Think of how many times you vaguely recall seeing an ad for a given product or service, but when it comes time to buy, you can't remember the name.

3.   They don't have a pressing need right now.

But next month they might, or the month after. The more often they see your name, the greater the likelihood they'll give you a call when they need your service.

4.   They are lazy.

They mean to give you a call but just don't get around to it. So, you have to keep reminding them.

5.   People may miss your ad.

No medium delivers 100% of its total audience at all times. But the more often you advertise, the better your chance of connecting.

6.   They have qualms about your business.

Maybe they heard something bad about you from a competitor or another customer. Over time that will fade from memory. Meantime, repetition tends to reinforce your message and reassure people that you are respectable.

7. People procrastinate.

They're too busy or lazy or preoccupied to call you now, but they count on seeing your ad again when they're in a better mood for making a buying decision.

8. They hesitate because of the expense.

They may not have the money now, but they may have it next week or next month. Some retailers are known to time certain ads so they appear right after the 1st and 15th of the month, when many people receive their paychecks.

9. They just patronized someone else.

But maybe they weren't satisfied with the service they received. Or maybe the other company will move away or close up shop. They could be receptive if they see your ad next time.

10. Your ad got reinforced by something they read.

The first time they saw your ad they weren't interested. But they just read an article about something you're selling and suddenly turn receptive.

When it comes to advertising, repetition works best. Repetition works best.

Solicit repeat business

It is much cheaper to retain existing customers than spend money on advertising to draw new ones. But you need to work at it. Keep a tickler file of past customers and target promotional literature to them. If someone who used to give you a lot of business doesn't anymore, give that person a call to find out why. Invest in low-cost promotional materials such as calendars, notepads and refrigerator magnets that constantly keep your name in front of past customers.

Solicit testimonials and referrals

If you're any good at what you do, from time to time you'll receive verbal compliments and on rare occasions written notes of praise. Treasure those testimonials. They are a mother lode of marketing value.

But don't wait for clients to take the initiative. No matter how satisfied they are with your performance, most are too busy or too lazy to take the time to write. Make it easy for them to offer testimonials and referrals. Every time clients make a verbal statement praising your work, follow up with a letter thanking them and asking for permission to quote them in your promotional materials. With written notes you already have the material on hand, but ask for permission to use it.

Promote ethnic advantages

Do you have anyone on staff fluent in a foreign language? Be sure to publicize this in all your promotional materials. (*Se habla español.*) Print business cards in both languages. This will give you the inside track for business in a given ethnic community.

Persistence pays off

A study reported by the Society for Marketing Professional Services found that 80% of all sales are made after the fifth call. Yet statistics show that 43% of salespeople make one call and quit, 25% make two calls and quit, and 12% quit after three calls.

You need to exercise good judgment with the old adage about not taking no for an answer. At some point people really do mean "NO!" and badgering them will just annoy them and waste your time. Just don't be too quick to come to that conclusion.

Speak so everyone understands

Businesses need to be multi-lingual. That is, they may use jargon when communicating with suppliers, co-workers and other business insiders, but they must learn to use simple, everyday language with their customers.

Chapter 9 – Capture Your Dreams!

You CAN Overcome The Obstacles

Some budding business owners may become disheartened after reading this book. As its title states, I've chosen to illuminate all the bumps in the road on the way to running a successful business. My goal is to provide a clear-eyed picture of those obstacles and, frankly, to discourage people who don't have the "right stuff" from hurting themselves, customers and capable competitors by starting enterprises that are doomed from the beginning due to lack of business acumen.

Another message needs to be emphasized, however. It's obvious that the obstacles detailed throughout these chapters CAN be overcome. A quick glance down any commercial street shows that it is possible to prevail. Millions of successful business owners have proven that business knowledge coupled with hard work and perseverance is a winning formula.

If they did it so can you. Here are some keys to success.

People, Money, Marketing.

Technical knowledge of a given field is a great starting point for a successful business, but not enough by itself. It needs to be supplemented by business knowledge focused on those three key areas cited earlier: People, Money, Marketing.

- Treat people – employees, customers, suppliers, and everyone else you encounter – the same way you'd want to be treated if the roles were reversed.
- Know your costs of doing business and constantly strive to lower expenses and boost revenues.

- Discover your Unique Selling Proposition(s) and market them to the hilt.

Many people have succeeded running a business they knew nothing about prior to starting or buying that business. Their gift is the ability to recognize opportunity in a lucrative market or one lacking sufficient coverage. Inevitably they acquire significant knowledge about the business as time passes but from the start all they could see was the opportunity to make money. They knew they could hire people with the requisite technical know-how while they focused on managing them, watching over the money and building clientele via their USPs.

Franchises generally have a higher success rate than competing independent businesses because they provide business knowledge and step-by-step operational guidance, no matter how little the franchisees may know about a particular business at the beginning. You don't have to be a restaurateur to buy a fast food franchise or an auto mechanic to own most of the auto repair franchises. All you need is the financing and a willingness to follow the franchise's business model. This speaks volumes about business knowledge trumping technical know-how.

Sell your value.

Certain businesses succeed with a marketing strategy based on low pricing – Wal-Mart being a prime example. They do that by running a tight ship, taking advantage of economies of scale and being enormously productive. However, most small businesses cannot hope to succeed as the lowest cost providers of their goods and services. Instead, they must sell value rather than price.

You may succeed by finding a niche in a market where price competition isn't very intense, or where customers are willing to pay more for top-quality goods and services. You may develop specialized goods or services, or a reputation for excellence that will result in customers seeking you out even if your prices are higher than most others in your field. Whatever the case may be, most successful small businesses entice customers to buy from them for reasons besides a low price.

Strive to own a business rather than a job.

It may seem counterintuitive, but one of the best things a business owner can do to insure success is to minimize his/her own importance to the business. This requires taking a cue from the franchises by developing detailed job descriptions, policies and procedures so that trusted people in the company can run it in your absence. This will accomplish two important things:

1. It will enable you to avoid burn-out by taking time off to enjoy the pleasures of life beyond running your business.

2. It will enable you to sell your business in the future if you decide to retire or do something else.

Many small businesses, maybe most of them, have their entire value based on the owner's know-how and contacts. Take away the owner and there's little left. These owners do no so much own a business as a job. Strive to own a business.

Love what you do.

Every successful business owner I've ever met radiated a passion for his/her work. Running a business can be difficult and filled with aggravation, but if you love what you're doing you'll find those difficulties and aggravations actually stimulating! You'll regard the bumps as challenges rather than obstacles.

An old saying goes:

If you love what you do for a living, you'll never work a day in your life!

That's how I felt about my calling, and that is the thought I want to leave you with in closing this book.

Yes, you CAN overcome those obstacles. And, you actually can have fun doing it.

Good luck in all of your endeavors.

--The End--

ABOUT THE AUTHOR

Jim Olsztynski (pronounced Ol-stin-skee) spent 34 years covering the plumbing-heating-cooling (PHC) industry as an editor and writer before retiring in August 2011. He was founding Editor of *Plumbing & Mechanical (PM)* magazine starting in 1984 and served as Editor/Editorial Director of PM until his retirement. From 2001-2011 he served simultaneously as Editor of *Supply House Times,* along with a two-year stint as Editor of *PM Engineer.* Additionally, Jim wrote a syndicated monthly column titled "Smart Business" that appeared in various construction industry magazines published by BNP Media Co. From 1993 until 2003, he published a multiple award-winning paid-subscription newsletter, *PHC Profit Report.*

Jim has served as a keynote speaker at dozens of PHC industry events, and has conducted seminars on business and promotional writing, small business marketing and various industry-related topics. He appeared on camera as a plumbing industry spokesperson for the History Channel's Modern Marvels 1997 program titled: "Arteries of Civilization: The History of Plumbing," which was based on PM's "History of Plumbing" series that ran in the magazine for a 10-year span. Throughout his career, Jim received more than two dozen awards for editorial excellence.

Since retiring, Jim has kept in touch with his former industry as a freelancer producing e-newsletters and blogs for the American Supply Association, Nexstar Network, Service Roundtable and private companies. He can be reached at wrdwzrd@aol.com.

Made in the USA
Monee, IL
03 September 2019